A small book with a BIG heart

LOVE notes

Words by Dr Andy Cope & Hannah Knowles

Brought to life by Amy Bradley

A small book with a BIG heart

L♥VE notes

Words by **Dr Andy Cope** & **Hannah Knowles**
Brought to life by Amy Bradley

CAPSTONE
A Wiley Brand

Registered Offices
John Wiley & Sons, Inc., 111 River Street, Hoboken, NJ 07030, USA
John Wiley & Sons Ltd, New Era House, 8 Oldlands Way, Bognor Regis, West Sussex, PO22 9NQ, UK

For details of our global editorial offices, customer services, and more information about Wiley products visit us at www.wiley.com.

The manufacturer's authorized representative according to the EU General Product Safety Regulation is Wiley-VCH GmbH, Boschstr. 12, 69469 Weinheim, Germany, e-mail: Product_Safety@ wiley.com.

Wiley also publishes its books in a variety of electronic formats and by print-on-demand. Some content that appears in standard print versions of this book may not be available in other formats.

Library of Congress Cataloging-in-Publication Data

ISBN 9781907312953 (Paperback)
ISBN 9781907312977 (ePdf)
ISBN 9781907312960 (ePub)

Cover Design: Amy Bradley

Set in 15/18pt Dreaming Outloud Sans by Straive, Chennai, India

Printed and bound in Great Britain by Bell & Bain Ltd, Glasgow

For DAISY

L O V E rules

This book comes with two simple rules:

Rule #1, you have to actually read it. Every sentence, every word. Slooooowly. No skimming.

When you've absorbed the messages, please think of someone you love, write their name on the next page, and move to rule #2 ...

Rule #2, you pass it on to that person. It's a pay-it-forward book. We're hoping that by the time you receive it, LOVE NOTES is frayed and tattered. That means it's been passed on and on and on and on (and on ...) in a chain of unadulterated love. The following page should be full of names, some you might know, others you don't.

If you are buying the book in mint condition, your job is to begin the chain. You've entered the love game at rule #1 which is super-thrilling because you are the love catalyst!

That sets you up nicely. As you're reading and absorbing the messages, you can be thinking about who you'll be passing LOVE NOTES onto.

Until then, it's 100% yours.

HAPPY READING!

I [*insert your name here..............................*]
am the LOVE CATALYST.

I am passing the book to

....

because I LOVE YOU!

I am passing the book to

....

because I LOVE YOU!

I am passing the book to

....

because I LOVE YOU!

I am passing the book to

....

because I LOVE YOU!

Bad news. I [*insert your name here*

....]

have got to buy a new book because this one's full! *Doh!* But good news, that makes me a LOVE CATALYST!

♥

KEEP
CALM
AND
START A
REVOLUTION

It's love, actually

Here's a challenge. We want you to organise these five things into priority order. No cheating or over-thinking, just total honesty.

In terms of importance to you (and they're all important!), how would you rank these five things:

Relationships. Success. Money. Happiness. Health.

1

2

3

4

5

I did the ranking activity with a bunch of 14-year-olds in Birmingham and they debated, argued and engaged. Some went for money as their priority *('Because, sir, if I had money I could buy all the others')* but most went for relationships, health or happiness.

We were about to move on when one of the lads raised his hand and said, *'Sir, you've missed something off the list.'*

I looked at the five words emblazoned on the screen and then back at the lad with a furrowed brow. *'What do you mean?'*

'Love, sir. If you add love to the list it changes everything.'

And 230 teenagers nodded in agreement. It's love, actually.

Ten Time Outs...

1. Meal time is delicious. *Savour it.*

2. Family time is important. *Cherish it.*

3. Friend time is limited. *Prioritise real ones.*

4. Partner time is massive. *Have fun!*

5. Children time is precious. *Be present.*

6. Play time is fun. *You're never too old to jump in puddles.*

7. Work time is enriching. *Add value.*

8. Alone time is abundant. *Like yourself.*

9. Down time is rejuvenating. *Schedule it.*

10. Now time is all you ever have. *Be in it.*

11. (BONUS) The time for LOVE is always. *BE love.*

Replaceable

A few years ago, I was working long hours, travelling around the country, hardly at home and not at all happy. Yet I couldn't stop.

It wasn't until I was having lunch with a friend when she honestly (and politely) said, *'You know, you are replaceable.'*

I sat there silently for a moment, wondering. I'm replaceable? Is that even true?

'It's not just you,' she reassured. *'We're all replaceable. Presidents, prime ministers, CEOs ... there's always someone else who will step in.'*

I sipped my fizzy water, pensively, as she delivered the killer line. *'Except, of course, with our loved ones.'*

I coughed up some fizz.

'Our family and our friends,' she said. *'To your closest few – your tribe – you are 100% irreplaceable.'*

Cue a lightbulb moment from me. She was absolutely right. Why was I spending all my time and energy doing a job that I really didn't enjoy that much? Double whammy – it was a job that was taking me away from my irreplaceable people and moments.

So I took a metaphorical deep breath and made a change. It did mean saying 'no' to some opportunities at work. There were a few awkward meetings and a short-term financial hit. But ultimately it meant saying 'yes' to precious family moments, time and opportunities I won't ever get back.

And you know what? I don't regret any of the business meetings, overnight stays, promotions and events I missed, because I was doing my other job. I'd committed to my most important role: being a good human – *being present* – to those that matter the most.

'I've realised
why we're here,'
whispered the boy.

'For cake?'
asked the mole.

'To love,'
said the boy.

'And be loved,'
said the horse.

(Charlie Mackesy, author of *The Boy*, *The Horse*, *The Raccoon*, *The Rabbit* and *The Mole*) [1]

[1] We reserve the right to get things mixed up.

Every day is a **Special** **PANTS** **day**

Life's too short.
QUIT waiting
for happiness

Unleash your special undies

It's our belief that everyone is a superhero but that too many people are *pretending* to be normal!

If you're going to swell the ranks of being an everyday superhero, you'll be needing some special pants.

So here's a favour you can do for yourself and your partner, right now ...

Pop upstairs to your bedroom and open your underwear drawer. In that drawer there will be some undies that you don't really fancy. If you're unsure which undies we're talking about, it's the misshapen, off-colour ones you wear when you're poorly. Or gardening.

We want you to identify these last-resort knickers/boxers and remove them from your drawer. Bin them, burn them or bury them in your garden so you never have to wear them again.

Because tomorrow, when you're showered, deodorised and getting dressed, you will open your underwear drawer and in there will be your 'special pants'. Once again, you know *exactly* which ones we mean.

And we want you to wear your special underwear for work tomorrow. That means when you pull up in the car park and stroll into work you will have a certain sparkle, a swagger and *je ne sais quoi* because you know what's cracking off down below.

Please note, our special pants top tip is not just a giggle. Positive psychology has a term – *enclothed cognition* – which means super-duper underwear is a legit way of making you feel good.

The sad fact is that on Monday morning most people's aim is to get through the week or survive until their next holiday. Humanity's in the collective habit of wishing our weeks away and placing happiness as a dot on the horizon.

Similarly, we tend to save our 'special pants' for a special occasion.

Here's a focusing fact: the average lifespan is 4,000 weeks. Life is a very short and precious gift. You've got 4,000 weeks to make a dent in the universe, so our 'special pants' top tip is simply a wake-up call.

It's a reminder to quit waiting.

Every day is a special pants day because LIFE is the ultimate special occasion.

#SpecialPants #EnclothedCognition #LoveNotes

The LOVE trilogy...

In a science overload, we're about to heap some psychology on top of the body of knowledge from the previous page to give you the best night out ever ...

Hedonism is about achieving a happiness high in double-quick time. Alcohol, chocolate and love are well-known happiness shortcuts, and while we're not recommending you overdose on them, they're pretty safe in moderation.

So, for your delectation, here's a wonderful study that brings these hedonistic shortcuts together in an explosion of love.

Boffins at the University of Bristol report that the key to long-term happiness is, erm, gardening.

Therefore, our mind-blowing LOVE combo is this:

On Friday night, why not wear your best undies, grab a bottle of red and a bar of choc in one hand, and the person you love with the other, and lead them down to the allotment ...

Mind. Blown!

RSPCY

Human beings are learning machines. We are fantastic at taking on new stuff.

But here's the thing, to upgrade to the best version of yourself you need to un-learn, and guess what? Human beings are really bad at *un-learning*.

Those beliefs and grudges, that inner critic, gnawing away inside your head – once you've invited them in, they make themselves right at home. These unwelcome visitors can become an infestation. If every cell in your body is eavesdropping on your inner dialogue, you really need to be careful what you say to yourself!

If you want to be the best version of yourself, a more loving and kinder human, then take a good look at some of the things you think and do and ask yourself the question: *Is this helpful or harmful?*

For example, holding onto a grievance is harmful. By not letting go of the past it is polluting your present moment.

So here's some wisdom from our brand new charity, the RSPCY ... the Royal Society for the Prevention of Cruelty to YOU.

It's easy to hold a grudge. But if you stop and think about it, who's that grudge really hurting?

There really is no situation where hatred helps. So be kind to yourself and *let go*. Remember, forgiveness is for *you*, not them! Choose love, always!

If you want any more persuading here are the words of Holocaust survivor Eva Kor:

'I forgive the Nazis not because they deserve it but because I deserve it.'

That's Eva Kor, people. Remember the name, and remember that forgiveness is for YOU.

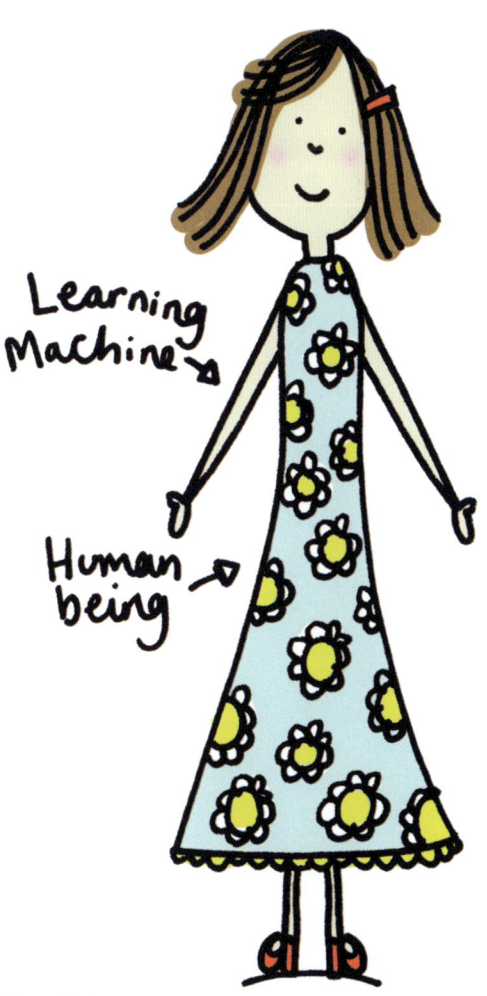

Learning Machine →

Human being →

If your definition of Success doesn't include love, get a better definition.

Humility isn't
thinking less of
yourself. It's thinking
of yourself, *less*.
Having less of you on
your mind.

Doppelgangers

Everyone knows that owners look like their dogs. We say it as a joke but science bears it out. It's because on a subconscious basis, we choose mutts that are similar to us.

Science has now taken the doppelganger theory further. Guess what, there's evidence to suggest that you may eventually grow to look like your partner?

No, really! Pinky promise. It's called *empathic mimicry*, and it's an actual thing.

Couples who live together for decades tend to have had the same experiences and spend a lot of time in rapport. This matching of emotions on the inside carves out facial features – frowns, anger, grumble mode, laughter lines, whatever – that show up on the outside.

Apparently, your facial muscles will be sculpted by time to match those of your long-term partner.

Empathic mimicry. Remember, you heard it here first.

The lesson?

Marry a <u>SMILER</u>

#EmpathicMimicry #LoveNotes

smile

Smiling is infectious,
you catch it like the flu. When someone smiled
at me today, I started smiling too.

I passed around the corner and someone saw
my grin. When he smiled I realised I'd passed it
on to him.

I thought about that smile, then I realised its
worth.
A single smile, just like mine could travel round
the earth.

So if you feel a smile begin, don't leave it
undetected. Let's start an epidemic quick and
get the world infected!

(Spike Milligan, comedian, actor, writer, poet)

LOVE-ability

Here are seven words that will change your life.

Do it better than you have to

And by 'it' we mean 'everything'.

Put more effort in than you have to.

Volunteer a bit more often than you have to.

Use your manners better than you have to.

Be a bit kinder than you have to.

Eat your veggies a bit better than you have to.

Be a better human (wife, partner, niece, nephew, teenager, sibling, parent, aunty, uncle, neighbour, friend, cousin, kid, grandparent, bestie, mum, dad, stepmum, stepdad, second cousin, great-grandparent, third cousin twice removed) than you have to.

... you get the point.

And the big one is, of course, LOVE a bit more than you have to. Give it, receive it, be open to it ... *be it!*

It's not about making dramatic changes. We're suggesting you start doing lots of little things a bit better than you did them yesterday. And tomorrow, a teensy weensy bit better again.

And again.

And again.

And again.

And again.

And again ...

It's about small improvements in attitude, behaviour and love-ability *every single day.* We think you'll really enjoy the upgrade and, guess what, these changes start to become normal, they get grooved into your habits and, hey presto, there's an *amaaaaaaaazing* person staring back at you while you brush your teeth.

Be the verb

REMINDER – a noun is a word that represents a person, thing or place, whereas a verb is a doing word.

Love often gets described as a noun, but it makes much more sense as a verb.

Oscar Wilde said we are not nouns, we are verbs, we are people who do things. In order to love better, we need to be the verb, not the noun.

Yep, deffo, 100%. Where love is concerned, *be the verb.*

Pretoogjes (Dutch):

'Fun eyes': the twinkling eyes
of someone engaging in benign
mischief or fun.

Duck for cover

There are phobias for everything.

We've cherry-picked a few of the obscure ones (which straight away will cause panic in the *kerasiphobic* community, who are afraid of cherries) ...

Fearful of feta? Panicked by parmesan? You're *turophobic* – terrified of cheese.

If you think your toaster's out to get you or that your microwave is looking at you in a funny way, you have *oikophobia* – the fear of kitchen appliances.

Arachibutyrophobia is the panicky thought of peanut butter sticking to the roof of your mouth.

The deliciously ironic *hippopotomonstrosesquipedaliophobia* is the fear of long words.

If you can have a
favourite fear, ours would
be *anatidaephobia*, the
irrational fear that
somewhere, a duck or goose is
watching you.

Then along came
phobophobia – the fear of developing a
phobia – which seems to trump them all.

Cheese, kettles, peanut butter, long words and
sinister mallards – they all seem a bit silly
unless you're a sufferer.

But here are two very serious and debilitating
fears ...

Cherophobia is the fear of happiness, and
philophobia is the fear of falling in love. It's
often triggered by not wanting your heart to
be broken, *again!*

Which begs the question: was Shakespeare
right? Is it better to have loved and lost, rather
than never loved at all?

Homo-sapien love

Men love women because they are the loveliest things on God's earth.

Women love men because chocolate can't mow the lawn.

Some men prefer to love other men.

Equally, some women prefer to love other women.

There is a word to describe this kind of behaviour ...

...LOVE.

(Guy Browning, author and humourist)

The LOVE child

Rewind to your birthday. Your *original* birthday. You, day one!

I'll spare you the graphic details in case you're reading this at breakfast time. Suffice to say, we all come into this world in the same way – naked, screaming and covered in gunge. (Note, if you exit the world in the same way, your relatives will be suing the care home).

Someone rubbed a sponge over you. Then you were wrapped in a towel and handed to your mum. In everyone else's eyes, you were a bald baby alien with bits of slime in your ears, but to your mum, you were the most beautiful thing in the entire world.

To be fair, you still are.

It was love at first sight. You to her, and her to you.

Which is a good job because I've just Googled the cost of raising a child. For the record, at the time of writing this book, a child comes with price tag of £223,356. 'Kid-flation' means this number rises daily.

Please note, £223,356 is the basic, no-frills, heating, clothes and food price. If we add in luxuries such as toys, haircuts, holidays, phones, trainers, games consoles and 15 years of education, it triples.

So, when your mum looked lovingly down at you and you gazed back, she was landing herself with a bill for a minimum of £223, 356.

That's LOVE, right there.

#Kidflation #LoveNotes

Give the gift of LIFE Available for pre-order. Best-seller. HUMAN BABY

All HUMAN BABY varieties come pre-programmed with unconditional love and arrive in rapid learning mode. HUMAN BABY can be programmed to speak any language. Adaptable to most environments. HUMAN BABY can be trained to walk and talk within ONE year and toilet-trained in two years (models vary).

Several skin tones to choose from. HUMAN BABY comes in traditional girl and boy models, or our brand new non-binary editions.

HUMAN BABY comes factory fitted with cuteness. Special features: chubby cheeks, gurgling, dribbling and fully squeezable thighs.

Order your HUMAN BABY today and get these extras:

- Sleep mode
- Awake mode
- Cry mode

(includes 'piercing scream', 'colic wailing' and 'cry for no reason' settings)

- Wide awake at 3 a.m. mode
- Nappy-filling mode
- Projectile vomiting mode
- Neurodiverse options are available

(enquire for spectrum details)

HUMAN BABY comes in various sizes. Standard delivery is nine months, but small ones can arrive early.

Starter price: £223,356

No refunds. No warranty. No questions asked. No training required. Luxuries (haircuts, toys, education, etc.) not included.

(Please leave a note if you're not in and we can leave HUMAN BABY with a neighbour.)

£223,356

(Taken from *The Art of Being BRILLIANT*)

'Love thy neighbour,
but be sure to draw the
curtains first.'

Philip Ardagh, author

LOVE Food

I suffer from a rare condition which causes me to wake up in the night, sneak down to the fridge and start eating. It's called insom-*nom*-*nom*-*nom*-*nom*-*nom*-nia.

To add weight to the problem, whoever invented food has made yummy food really fattening and salad-y food really slimming. If I'd been the food inventor, I'd have made it the other way round. But, hey, food is what it is.

YUMMY! And MOREISH!

The official advice on food yo-yos: one week red wine and dark chocolate are good for you (Yay!), then they're dropped in favour of Tibetan spring water and kale (Boo!).

So, to help you LOVE food and your body, here are our modern-day DOs and DON'Ts for eating properly, having energy and living forever.

✓ DO live by the Japanese mantra *Hara hachi bu*, which literally translates as *'stop eating just before you're full'*. *Hara hachi bu* takes a bit of getting used to because it means you don't have to stuff your face. It's okay to leave something. Your stomach is about the size of your fist (one fist, not both!).

I mean, who knew?

✓ DO sit down and eat as a family (as often as possible). If it's not happening, insist that it does.

✓ DO understand that *how* you eat is as important as *what* you eat. Switch off the TV and implement a mealtime phone ban. Chat instead. In Spain, *sobremesa* is the relationship-rich time after you've finished eating but before you get up from the table. It's high-quality time spent in conversation – connecting, relaxing, enjoying, debating and talking nonsense.

✓ DO appreciate your food. That means savouring it and thanking whomever provided it. That might be God but, more likely, J Sainsbury.

DON'T eat in front of a screen or standing up. ✗

✓ DO eat fast food. But *sloooowly*, and occasionally. Once you understand that the 's' in fast food is a silent 's', you begin to make better food choices. That means these sub-rules automatically follow:
a) DON'T eat without cutlery or out of a box. ✗
b) DON'T eat anything delivered to your door by someone on a motorbike. ✗
c) DON'T eat anything passed to you in your car through a hatch. ✗
d) DON'T eat anything your great-great-grandma would not have recognised as food. ✗

✓ DO cook from scratch where possible. Or marry someone who can.

✓ DO go for a stroll after your meal. βόλτα or volta (originating from Modern Greek) is an expression that literally means *'let's go a turn'* and is similar to the English saying *'let's stretch our legs'*. More precisely it can translate as *'evening promenade'*, and the term is translated in Italian as *passeiggiata*. While local expressions differ across Europe, it widely refers to the hours of the evening, around dusk, where locals go for a stroll around town.

This tradition has a distinctly Mediterranean feel of meandering around seaside towns as the sun sets on the horizon. Yes, it's more difficult to replicate after you've scoffed your tea in Rochdale, but why not give it a whirl.

Yummy words

If you LOVE food, you'll LOVE these words:

Guaranteed you'll have experienced *uitbuiken* (Dutch; literally 'out-bellying') which is that belt-loosening, post-Sunday lunch bloated feeling.

Shemomedjamo (Georgian) is a variation on the above. You know when you're really full, but your meal is just so delicious, you can't stop eating it? The Georgians feel your pain. Shemomedjamo literally means *'I accidentally ate the whole thing'.*

Fika (from Sweden) is all about taking it slow, and pausing for downtime and maybe having a laid-back chat over coffee. The working day and even the school day may be interrupted twice for a *fika* coffee/cake diversion. Note, *fika* is absolutely NOT about grabbing a coffee and drinking it on the go through the stupid little sipping hole. It's a deliberate act of stopping, sitting, chatting and relaxing.

Our final note on LOVING food is this simple reminder: there were people on the Titanic who turned down the sweet trolley. The learning ...

... always say yes to a pudding!

... the older I get, the
more I realise how
much I LOVE being
at HOME doing
nothing.

Piglet:
'How do you spell love?'

Pooh Bear:
'You don't spell it ... you feel it.'

(A. A. Milne, author)

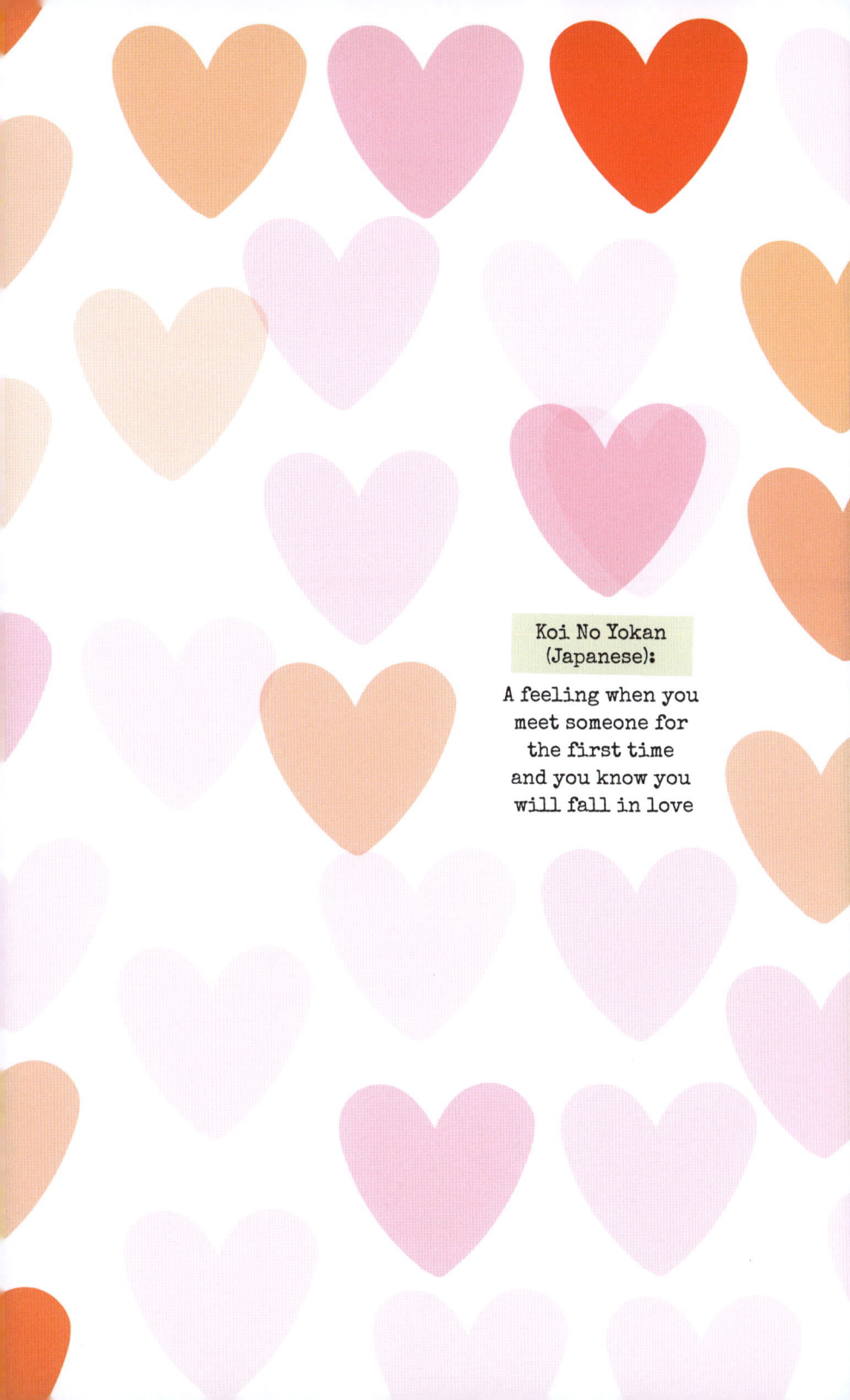

Koi No Yokan (Japanese):

A feeling when you meet someone for the first time and you know you will fall in love

Learning to LOVE insults

When someone says something nasty, before you retaliate and wound with your words, remind yourself of this – *it's hurt people who hurt people.*

So instead of adding to the vicious cycle, the best thing you can do is throw a lifeline of love.

Or, if that's beyond you, try this top tip from two and a half thousand years ago.

Context: if you've seen pictures of the Buddha, you'll notice his yo-yoing weight.
Sometimes he was large and sometimes stick thin, so here's us, reading between the lines ...

One day, someone insulted the Buddha. We're not sure what was said but, if this was a betting game, our money's on it being said when he was in his 'large' phase.

Buddha thought about the insult and then said to the guy, *'If you give a gift and the gift isn't accepted, who does the gift belong to?'*

The insulter furrowed his brow. *'The person who owns it, I guess?'*

And cooler than a refrigerated cucumber, the Buddha retorts, *'I'm not accepting the insult. So who now does it belong to?'*

Take from that what you will. *Right back atcha* from the little/big/little/big man.

LIFE: THE SMALL PRINT

When your mum agreed to the basic idea of birthing you, she signed you up to a contract called 'LIFE'. But your mum didn't scroll through the reams of small print. The old girl did what everyone does: she whizzed through and ticked the 'I agree' box at the end.

But we've unearthed the original contract. We're not going to bore you with all 176 pages of small print, but it's worth reviewing the basic terms and conditions that come with the deal we call 'LIFE'.

We thought you might like a few snippets of the original Ts & Cs:

1. LIFE is available for a limited time only.

2. LIFE comes with NO guarantees and absolutely NO refunds.

3. LIFE is not fair. (See clauses 1 & 2.)

4. Grumbling that LIFE is not fair is therefore true, but pointless.

5. LIFE comes with only one rule: sometimes you just have to suck it up. (See clauses 2–4.)

6. The length of LIFE is variable. If you look after yourself you might experience an extended warranty. Note: 'might'. (See clauses 1, 2 & 3.)

7. Finding happiness and LOVE is the sole responsibility of the user. The management shall not be held responsible for the user failing to find happiness and/or LOVE. (See clauses 2 & 3.)

8. LIFE is subject to change without notice.

9. LIFE is lived alongside other people who've also signed up to this contract. Their LIFE contract might appear to be better than yours but everyone gets the exact same terms and conditions. The difference is that they've realised and accepted clauses 1–8.

10. 'LIFE' is best lived loved.

LOVE poetry

It doesn't interest me what you do for a living.
I want to know what you ache for and if you dare
to dream of meeting your heart's longing.

It doesn't interest me how old you are.
I want to know if you will risk looking like a
fool for love, for your dream, for the adventure
of being alive.

It doesn't interest me who you know or how you
came to be here.
I want to know if you will stand in the centre of
the fire with me and not shrink back.

It doesn't interest me where or what or with whom
you have studied.

I want to know what sustains you from the inside
when all else falls away. ... I want to know if you
can be alone with yourself and if you truly like
the company you keep in the empty moments.

(Extracts from 'The Invitation' by Oriah Mountain Dreamer)

Expecting the world to treat you fairly because you are a NICE person is like expecting a bull NOT to charge because you are a vegan.

The break-up survival guide

We have all had our hearts broken. Whether you have been broken up with or whether you were the one doing the breaking up, it usually involves the same formula: tears, hours of brooding, consuming your bodyweight in chocolate and an achy-breaky heart.

Elisabeth Kübler-Ross shared the five stages of grief which describe the emotional journey we go on when we are grieving the loss of a loved one. This model has since gone to explain change and is widely used in businesses.

We have decided to put our own spin on the Kübler-Ross model to support you the next time you are going through the emotional rollercoaster that is a break-up.

Denial

This is the stage when our grip on reality is a little shaky. We might find ourselves saying things like, 'They will realise they have made a mistake ... They will come crawling back, just you wait.' In the denial stage we might find ourselves doing things we didn't think we would ever do like stalking them online or 'accidentally' bumping into them in the local supermarket. We tell anyone who'll listen that we're just on a break and that they just need some space ... from real love, apparently.

Song for this stage: 'It Wasn't Me' – Shaggy

Anger

This is where we find ourselves saying things like, 'They had the best years of my life ... I wasted my youth on that emotionless lump.' We might rage-text our bestie and insist on throwing away anything that has had anything to do with them or anything they may have touched. We might find ourselves being drawn to the kickboxing class at the gym or hear our friends tell us that the vein in our forehead is bulging ... again.

Song for this stage: 'Go Your Own Way' – Fleetwood Mac

Bargaining

We read books about people who have come back from tough times, we watch every romcom ever made, we flirt with the idea of sending them a casual message at 3 a.m. We talk to whoever will listen, even if that includes our cat, and try to find ways of negotiating the situation. We ask for advice, but we don't act on any of it; in fact, we do the opposite of what we have been told.

Song for this stage: 'Let's Stay Together' – Al Green

Depression

Here we might find ourselves withdrawing from the outside world, we keep the curtains drawn, and the only people we are speaking to are the local takeaway via an app. In this stage, we find ourselves being drawn to anything chocolate flavoured because we all know calories don't count during a break-up. Carbs become our support group.

Song for this stage:

'Total Eclipse of the Heart' – Bonnie Tyler

Acceptance

At some point, we will find ourselves waking up on the sofa where we have lived for the last week, with popcorn stuck to our cheek (often glued by the tears that haven't stopped flowing). It is usually at this point when we give ourselves a good talking to and think it's time to work on our 'revenge body'. We might begin to venture outside again, but probably wearing sunglasses. Welcome to the acceptance stage.

Song for this stage: 'I Will Survive' – Gloria Gaynor

♥

Peace and Love

The Hippy Code ...

Do your own thing, wherever you have to do it, and whenever you want. Drop out. Leave society as you have known it. Leave it utterly. Blow the mind of every straight person you can reach. Turn them on, if not to drugs, then to beauty, love, honesty and fun.

We'll inhale to that!

#HippyCode #LoveNotes

Who taught you this...

Monday

Tuesday

Wednesday

Thursday

Friday

Happy Choose Day

Choosing to carry an attitude that works in your favour is a massive power-up. And it's always choose day!

Here are some positive choices that you can start making, right now:

Choose progress over perfection.

Choose courage over fear.

Choose responding positively over-reacting negatively.

Choose losing and learning over winning and celebrating.

Choose optimism over pessimism.

Choose you over trying to be someone else.

Choose acceptance over judgement.

Choose hard work over an easy life.

Choose doing what's right over doing what's easiest.

Choose botheredness over can't-be-botheredness.

Choose kindness over meanness.

Choose Mondays over Fridays.

Choose giving it a go over giving up.

Choose personal responsibility over blaming others.

Choose opening your eyes rather than rolling your eyes.

But most of all,

choose LOVE

over anything else.

#ChooseDay #LoveNotes

When you choose fear, love appears not to be enough; but when you choose love, it can help you heal every fear.

(Robert Holden, author and speaker)

Every buzz in my pocket, I hope it's your name.

(Modern romance from Conan Gray, 'Telepath')

A top tip from the happiest country in the world...

While going out to drink with friends might be fun, it's also expensive, exhausting and oftentimes you end up drinking more than you originally bargained for, which ruins your tomorrow.

In Finland you can treat yourself to a *kalsarikännit* (pronounced kal-sari-kaneet) night in. Stylised to 'päntsdrunk', *kalsarikännit* translates as *'drinking at home in your underwear with no intention of going out'.*

#PANTSdrunk

Oh, those cheeky Fins!

If we look beyond the humour, pantsdrunk is one more way to celebrate the importance of relaxation. It's an attitude and philosophy that starts from inner peace. It's not really about excessive alcohol at all; it's about taking time out, indulging in a little of what you enjoy and being authentic.

Best of all, pantsdrunk does not require expensive furniture, artisanal hot chocolate, scented candles or a gluten-free cushion – just your drink of choice, a comfy sofa and a TV show you're happy to binge-watch.

Sounds like the perfect weekend! If you're going to indulge in pantsdrunk we recommend that:
a) you draw the curtains before you start, and
b) you turn up the thermostat a degree or two

Lots of lifestyle trends tell you to switch off your phone and get outside. Wouldn't you rather be inside with a bottle of lager, working your way through a series on Netflix?

Semi-naked?

Hey, if it works for the world's happiest people, it might be worth a spin?

#PantsDrunk #LoveNotes

TOP TIP:

Be a good friend.

To yourself.

Secrets to living a long and fulfilling life:

♥ scroll half

♥ walk double ♥

♥♥♥ laugh triple

♥♥♥♥ love quadruple

Dear Smartphone

You need to understand that I love you. I always have and I always will. But I'm going to have to walk away, so this is my break-up letter (I did consider writing it as a text message but that would be too ironic).

We've had such joyous times and shared some amazing videos. And yet somehow, over the past few months something's not felt right. Our relationship's become complicated. *You've* become complicated! Plus, you never leave me alone. All those reminders, emails, notifications and WhatsApp groups. And your constant buzzing. Even in the night!

Cutting to the chase, there's only so long that I can stay in an abusive relationship. My relationship with you has been so full-on that I've neglected the important people in my life. I sit in the same room as them but I'm not *with* them, I'm with you; scrolling, swiping, double-thumbing, liking, poking, commenting, checking, following. And when I'm with you, I'm *absent* from them, which is neither right nor fair.

It's not just at home. When I'm at the cinema, I'm with you, scrolling during the slow bits. I sneak you into meetings, I'm with you on the train, and we always go to the loo together.

Me and thee, sometimes we can spend a whole 8 hours thumb to screen. That's 50% of my entire waking life. And when I'm with you my actual real life is passing by. Recently I started to add up the hours and it made me scared.

Scared of the things I *won't* have done, the sights I didn't see, the moments that passed me by and the people I neglected to spend time with. I need to commit time to the *real* people in my life. The flesh and blood ones. Those closest to me. Those who often sit in the same room as me, thumbing their phones while I thumb you.

I'm breaking up with you so I can commit to them.

So I'm proposing that we cool it. As I said at the outset, it's not lack of love. I love you. I'll always love you, but I need some time and space to get my head together. I'm suggesting we cut down our time together by 75%.

I already know I'll miss you and I'm certain to be tempted so it's got to be mutual. You've got to agree to me switching off *all* notifications and *all* alerts, deleting loads of apps, and ...

... I'm not sure how to say this ...

... *we need to sleep in separate bedrooms.*

No more between-the-sheets action. That bit's over for good. I know. I'm so sorry. I can actually feel tears welling. You're going to have to agree to sleep on the sofa or in the spare room. You can't be the last thing I see at night and the first thing my bleary eyes lock onto in the morning. It's not healthy.

You say you're all about freedom, but you're not. I feel trapped. You say you're all about connection, but you're not. I feel lonely.

I've got a life that needs living, *fully.* That means I'm truly committed to less *you* time and more *me* time. Because I know that a better me is the key to better relationships with my family and friends.

Thanks for the memories.

X

(Adapted from *LADULT: Navigating Safely from Boy to Man*
by Andy & Ollie Cope)

'Money can buy you a fine dog, but only love can make him wag his tail.'

(Kinky Friedman, American singer, songwriter, novelist and politician)

LOVE on the rocks

If you're ever in Antarctica and you hear a wild trumpeting sound, chances are it'll be a Gentoo penguin. In actual fact you're more likely to hear a fanfare of trumpeting because Gentoos are social creatures – they hang around in colonies of peace, love and kindness.

Gentoos aren't just social, they're also very romantic. Like many of their penguin relatives, Gentoos form deep and lasting bonds with their chosen partners and are known to mate for life. But what sets them apart is their heartwarming way of expressing their love: 'pebbling'.

During the breeding season, a male Gentoo penguin will spend hours searching for the smoothest, most perfect pebble he can find. He presents this pebble to his desired mate as a token of his affection. If she accepts, the pebble becomes the foundation of their nest and symbolises the beginning of their life together.

It's quite beautiful.

The learning?

Maybe we can do away with expensive engagement rings and lavish gifts. Get yourself down to Brighton Beach, choose the smoothest pebble, and present it to your loved one. Explain about pebbling. Maybe make some sort of trumpeting sound? Tell them it's the thought that counts!

#Gentoo #Pebbling #LoveNotes

Love lessons from the animal kingdom

We have heard about the romantic nature of penguins, but they aren't the only winged creatures in the animal kingdom that are romantics at heart.

Take bowerbirds, the unsung artists of the avian world. Male bowerbirds build intricate 'bowers' (basically a leafy art installation) to woo females. They decorate these nest-like structures with attention-grabbing items like berries, feathers, flowers and even bottlecaps. These interior designers get quite obsessed and sort each item by shape and hue and have no problem stealing charms from a neighbouring structure if it will improve their chances. They even practise 'optical illusions' to make their bowers appear bigger and more symmetrical. It is then up to the female to inspect these masterpieces and decide which

one tickles her fancy. Once she is inside the show home, the male proceeds to perform a dance while holding a favourite trinket in his beak, hoping to seal the deal.

It's not just the bowerbirds that like a boogie, the Galapagos albatross perform elaborate mating dances that can take years to perfect. The performance will include lots of head swaying, bill clacking and moving in sync. This is more than just a fun time for these birds, this is an audition to let Fred Astaire know that he has found his Ginger Rogers. Once the dance is over, they become a monogamous pair that lasts their entire 60-year lifespan. Hey, they aren't called lovebirds for nothing.

A different expression of love comes from the porcupine. Male porcupines spray urine on potential mates as part of their courtship. If the female enjoys the urine shower, they become a match. If being covered in wee isn't her thing, she chases him away.

Take what works and leave what doesn't.

Pet names

For most couples, there comes a point on their relationship journey when they enter the 'pet name phase'. This usually happens after one does a romantic gesture or you finally let your guard down and eat spaghetti in front of each other.

It often starts innocently enough: Honey, Babe, Love, Sweetie ... all of these are okay to use in public and you won't find any raised eyebrows or snorts when addressing your significant other in front of the in-laws.

But these pet names are a slippery slope. One minute you have your mother-in-law's approval, the next your dignity is in question when you accidentally address her daughter as 'Doodlebug'.

You see, these names mutate in a very short space of time. They get lengthened, shortened and turned into names that are so ridiculous and unrecognisably human.

'Bub' becomes 'Bubs', then 'Lob Butt', then before you know it you are whispering sweet nothings to your beloved 'Lobster Butter'.

'Boo' turns into 'SupBoo', and finally morphs into 'Supreme Burrito'.

Captain Cuddleface

'Pookie' quickly becomes 'Pooks', then 'Pookster', and ultimately you become known as 'The Pookinator'.

So, unless you want to be known to your friends and family as 'Captain Cuddleface' or 'Schmoopy von Snugglepants', choose your pet names wisely.

What
happened
today
that
made
your

heart
do a
little
DANCE?

The seven GREAT wonders of the world

1. To see

2. To hear

3. To touch

4. To taste

5. To feel

6. To laugh

7. ... and to LOVE ❤️

HEALTH
WARNING!

Being in love can give you shortness of breath, palpitations and an inability to concentrate.

The exact same symptoms as carbon monoxide poisoning.

Types of LOVE

AGRAPE
Love for humanity

PHILAUTIA
Self-love

PRAGMA
Love that lasts

MANIA
All-consuming love

EROS
Romantic love

PHILIA
Love between friends

STORGE
Familial love

LUDUS
Playful love

Dr Feelgood

Yes, medication and therapy might fix things but here are the 10 best doctors in the world.

1. Outdoors

2. Rest

3. Exercise

4. Healthy diet

5. Self-confidence

6. Friends

7. Sleep

8. Happiness

9. Time

10. Love

11.

12.

Feel free to arrange them in the order of importance to you.

Oh, and we've left space for you to add two more 'doctors' who will repair and rejuvenate you.

I rebel by :LOVING: more

Yung Pueblo, poet

If I love myself
I love you.
If I love you
I love myself.

(Rumi, poet and scholar from way back)

Be your own cheerleader

Beware, self-love can go too far ...

Narcissus was a Greek mythological heart-throb. One fine day he looked in a pool, saw his reflection and fell madly in love. Yes, with himself!

Imagine, being that gorgeous, *and that stupid?*

Long story short, it didn't end well for Narcissus and his story serves as a cautionary tale about being self-obsessed and/or self-important (i.e., narcissistic).

We're not advocating that you take self-love to the attention-seeking level of 'look at me, I'm so much better than everyone else'. Because, truthfully, you're not! We're suggesting that you flip your identity away from being your own worst enemy, towards being your own bestie.

An admirer instead of a critic.
An ally instead of an adversary.
A cheerleader instead of a heckler.

Cut the pouting, preening and posing because, in the words of Abi Roberts (comedian and writer), 'People who use selfie sticks really need to have a good, long look at themselves.'

LOVE social media

Would you rather: Take a selfie or go swimming with sharks?

FACT: There have been 379 selfie-related deaths in the last 13 years. These include fatal falls from cliffs, accidents with cars and trains, dangerous wildlife encounters and unforeseen drownings.[2]

During the same period, only 90 people have been killed by sharks.

Which brings us to some questions worth pondering:

1. Is social media more dangerous than swimming with sharks?

2. Is social media making us anti-social?

3. Instead of bringing communities together, has social media created a divide?

[2] It's gonna be way more than 379. According to a study by the *Journal of Family Medicine and Primary Care*, selfie-related deaths are most likely underreported as they are not usually listed as the cause of death.

A real friend →

↰ the flesh & blood type!!

4. Are we too busy chasing followers instead of real-life flesh and blood friends?

5. Do we scroll through everyone else's highlight reel and feel jealous, inadequate and unloved?

Don't misunderstand. We're not suggesting social media is bad. It's just that we're not suggesting that it's good either. It's nothing really – without you. It really is what you choose to make of it.

So, in a LOVE NOTES world exclusive, we emailed Yoda (no, really, we did!) and asked Oh Green One to pen a few pearls of internet wisdom. Here are Yoda's six tips to gaining enlightenment and becoming a Jedi Master of online love.

It's strange that he can be so wise, yet his English is so awful!

Anyhow, here's what he said:

1. Absolute truth online, there is not. The loudest and angriest gets heard, but correct this does not make them. Often, very wrong they are. Search engines – what you want, they give. Not what you need, it is. Your truth, the only truth, it is not.

2. Online, anything you share, haunt you it will.

A friendly ghost or a nightmare, it might be. The internet never forgets, remember.

3. When the fun stops, STOP you must! In control of your screen usage, remain you must, or control you it will. Know your limits, set them, and stick to them you must.

4. At their phone 150 times a day, the average person looks. Much looking there is, but not necessarily finding. Too much to see there is. Surf we do, riding one superficial peak to another, without diving into the depths. Breadth of knowledge, good it is, but depth of understanding, just as important.

5. Health warning, this is! Excessive screen time, junk living it is. A domino effect, there is. Junk living to junk sleeping leads to junk eating and to junk relationships. Good it is not!

6. Estimated, it is, that 61% of people have texted someone in the same room. Ringing alarm bells should be. Why? Social animals, human beings are. A team effort, evolution has been. The test of time, together you've stood. Divided, fallen you have. Energise each other, you do. Texting someone in the same room, the behaviour of an anti-social animal it is. Go chat, smiles make, eye contact, love, advice good.

Your secret place

Picture a place where you can go and nobody will know you're there – or, if they do, they'll know not to bother you. It's a place you can go to when you're stressed or tired or overwhelmed.

Smultronställe (Swedish, pronounced smul-tron-stelle), meaning 'wild strawberry patch', symbolises your happy place. It's not a literal patch of strawberries, it's the perfect retreat where you go to escape the world. A shady grove, perhaps; or a quiet spot in a nearby park; a favourite café or even your own back garden.

It is an underrated, low-key gem of a place, often with sentimental value, that just makes you feel better.

Where's your *#smultronställe?*

And while we're in Scandinavia, let's hop over to Denmark and introduce one of our favourite concepts: *Hygge.*

Hygge has no direct English translation. It's been described as the pursuit of everyday happiness, being consciously cosy, enveloped in snuggliness or our personal favourite – socialising for introverts.

Hygge is all about good food, atmosphere, being together with the people you love, relaxing, gratitude and contentment. Hygge teaches that wonderful, loving moments are there for the taking in our everyday lives; we just need to slow down enough to notice.

One of the best things about hygge is that it's not about money. It's grounded in simplicity. For example, sitting with your family on a rickety picnic bench, in the drizzle, eating slightly soggy sandwiches and sharing a flask of soup is more hygge than having those same people in a fancy-pants restaurant, drinking expensive wine and eating unpronounceable food.

Hygge allows us to snuggle into our everyday environments and luxuriate in the beautiful ordinary.

Best of all, hygge creates connection with the people we love the most.

The language of LOVE

There's a magic number that keeps relationships fresh. It's called the Losada ratio. If you Google it you'll find it's one of those things that's been proven, disproven, re-proven and batted around a few times, but we like it because it's simple, free and it works.

For relationships to survive, you should be three times more positive than you are negative. Note, the ratio is 3:1, not 3 to zero, so you can be grumbly and negative if you wish, but every time you say something negative or critical, you should balance it up with 3 positives.

That's 3 bits of praise, 3 bits of encouragement, 3 bits of good news, 3 thank-yous, 3 catching people doing things well and telling them ...

3:1 is the *minimum* you should be aiming for.

To create really strong buzzing relationships, your positive to negative ratio should be 6:1. That's 6 bits of praise, encouragement, good news, thank-yous and nice comments about people behind their back.

We're not asking you to be stupidly positive and praise people for nothing. The 6:1 ratio is about listening back to yourself and consciously calling out the good instead of lazily pointing out the bad. Try these for size:

I love you

Great work

Thanks so much

What a lovely smile

I love your positivity

That's amazingly kind

You've been so helpful

Thanks for being on time

I love having you on the team

Dad, you do the world's best fried eggs

I adore that scarf, where did you get it from?

If you cup your ear and listen you'll hear a lot of people doing the exact opposite. There will be six grumbles for every positive!

Remember, LOVE NOTES is about setting a high bar. It'll be higher than those around you. Be honest. Listen back to yourself. If you want to create strong relationships, six positives for every negative is the language of love.

Love NOW!

We pay thousands for a smartphone to ensure we're never bored. Our scrolling is powered by FOMO and yet the biggest irony is that by scrolling we *are* missing out.

We're missing the moment.

We're missing eye contact.

We're missing nature.

We're missing out on actual real life.

Bringing your whole self to the present moment is quite a thing. It means you've engaged with life. Absolutely.

Imagine - life is playing out right now and you're not showing up. You've got a Willy Wonka golden ticket, an entry to the biggest prize of them all - LIFE - and you can't find the entrance.

Imagine NOT rocking up to the biggest moment in history - THIS ONE.

The present moment. It's a gift! Embrace the sumptuousness of now. Unwrap the moment. Delve in. Smother yourself in now-ness.

Oh, and the 'delve in' rule applies even if it's stressful, or difficult or boring. Don't reject the moment because it's not perfect. It might not be exactly as you want, but it's all you've got.

Make the most of what you've been given.

Love now because NOW is all you have. It's the key to being all of you. It opens you up to loving life.

The Bank of TIME

Imagine waking up to find that you have £86,400 in your bank account. *WooHoo!*

But here's the catch: at the end of the day no balance is carried over. At midnight, every night, the bank will delete the remaining amount in your account.

Knowing this, what would you do?

The answer is obvious – withdraw every penny!

We all own an account like this. It is from The Bank of TIME.

Every morning, we are credited with 86,400 seconds. Every evening, whatever is left in the account is gone forever. You can never use more than the 86,400 and you certainly can't move them into the next day.

You need to use the day's deposit, otherwise it is lost.

Beware those pesky clocks. They're watching, tick-tocking, 86,400 times a day.

The trouble is, we aren't very good at valuing time. We easily waste an awful lot of these precious seconds every day. So here's a thought experiment ...

To know the value of one year, ask the prisoner waiting for their sentence to end.

To know the value of one month, ask the mother who gave birth to her baby prematurely.

To know the value of one week, ask the person waiting for their test results.

To know the value of one hour, ask a child who is playing with their friends.

To know the value of one minute, ask the person who has just missed their flight.

To know the value of one second, ask the person who has just avoided an accident.

We need to start appreciating these moments because once they are gone, they are gone forever.

The paradox of time – the faster you race, the further you are from the present moment.

Love is the drug, and you are the dealer ...

Humans are built to certain specifications that enable them to withstand the normal wear and tear of life, but remember the pressures of the modern world are considerable.

People do actually break – and that's fine. It's to be expected. Your family and friends don't come with a receipt. If they're wilting under the strain, or if they have developed a fault, or have actually broken, you can't take them back to the shop and swap them for a new one.

But here's a sure-fire 100% guaranteed way to help fix a broken friend, sibling or parent.

You must put the love back into their hearts.

First, if it was you who caused them to break, say sorry and mean it. That will help you and them to move on and put whatever 'it' was behind you. And that's where you need to leave all your troubles – in the past.

Based on the fact that sometimes it's easier to show love than to say it, here's a little extra something in your love repair kit ... the magical seven-second hug. Note, the average hug lasts 2.1 seconds, so 7 seconds is really stretching it. Which is exactly the point. Sometimes your loved ones need a pick-me-up, so a seven-second hug, plus an 'I love you' and/or 'I'm sorry and I mean it', is a wonderful explosion of genuine affection. It heals almost anything.

#HugDealer

If you don't believe us, put the book down, go do a seven-second hug, and come back. Oh, nearly forgot, if you're going to be a hug dealer, it's important to read the small print on the next page ...

Hug Dealer small print

Seven seconds is an I ♥ U hug. No words are necessary. Seven seconds is just long enough for the other person to know that you love them. It contains life-changing properties but should only be administered to very close family and friends. It's absolutely NOT for strangers in the park because that would be weird. Never count out loud because it spoils the effect. You don't actually have to wait for your siblings, parents, gran or bestie to look jaded before you do the seven-second hug thing. They provide an instant boost pretty much anytime. Warning: seven seconds is advanced hugging. Those who are already huggy will absolutely love the full seven seconds, but you'll be able to spot the non-huggers – they start wriggling and you have to cling on for the love to transfer. Good luck!

#HugDealer #7SecondHugging #LoveNotes

(Borrowed from *The Art of Being a Brilliant Teenager* by Andy Cope and Amy Bradley)

There's a
WONDERFUL
form of therapy
that's good for
healing almost
EVERYTHING

It's called LOVE.

Love Mummy Earth

Love extends beyond people, to animals, property and your environment, including old Mother Earth herself.

She's been kind enough to provide us with a delicate ecosystem. We're in the Goldilock's zone, just far enough from the sun not to burn alive but close enough for warmth. Just the right gaseous mixture to create breathable air. Just enough of an ozone layer to protect against deadly solar radiation. This big bang of local circumstances has enabled millions of species of flora, fauna and life to co-exist.

But it's a very delicate balance.

This last century has seen us take a wrecking ball to our planet. Our relationship with Mother Earth is that we're takers, not givers. As a species, we're single-handedly altering the planet's chemical, biological and physical balance. It's safe to say that if people got wiped out, all other species would benefit enormously. With the human wrecking ball gone, the biosphere would breathe a sigh of relief (literally!). Forests would regenerate, oceans would clean themselves, fish stocks would recover, the air would purify and orangutans would move into our deserted tower blocks.

I'm not asking you to take personal responsibility for all of it, just your bit. Which means falling back in love with your home planet.

This is easier said than done because the global party lights are flashing and it can be difficult to resist a Golden Ticket to the materialist party.

But rather than accepting the Golden Ticket and joining the party that's dancing itself to death, we think there's a better alternative.

The solution? Instead of changing the climate outside, why not change it inside with peace, contentment and a bit of spiritual enlightenment. The enlightened woo-woo bit begins with a massive shift of thinking. *Once you've got enough, then you'll be content* never works, because you'll never have enough. It pays to switch the sentence to the slightly weird truth, which reads: *once you're content, you'll have enough.*

To do your bit for Mummy Earth, you need to learn to love what you already have and who you already are. Quitting the chase is good for you, and her.

Paws for Thought[3]

Half-true story. I once had an imaginary conversation with a dog. It was deep, and it went like this ...

I have never been to the greyhound races, but I have seen them on television. They have these amazing dogs wearing snazzy jackets who chase a mechanical rabbit around the track. When the dogs get to the point that they can no longer race, the owners put a little ad on greyhound.com to see if anybody wants to adopt one as a pet. If no one takes them, the dogs are destroyed.

My Uncle Geoff can't stand the thought of the greyhounds being destroyed, so he adopts them. He has several of these big old greyhound dogs hanging around his very small house. Geoff loves them.

Once, when I was at Uncle Geoff's, a big spotted greyhound called Charlie was lying there in his basket. One of the kids in the family, just a toddler, was pulling on Charlie's tail, and a slightly older kid had his head on the big dog's rib cage, using it for a pillow.

Charlie didn't seem to mind. In fact, despite being tormented, he was wearing a big satisfied doggy smile.

I said to Charlie, *'You still racing, mate?'*

'Nah,' the dog said. *'Gave it up.'*

'Do you miss the glitter and excitement of the track?' I asked.

[3] Adapted from Fred Craddock, "But What About the Weeds?" in *The Cherry Log Sermons* (Louisville: Westminster John Knox Press, 2001).

Charlie lifted his head to look at me. 'Not at all,' he said.

'Why did you stop? Did you get too old to race?'

'Gosh no, I had plenty more racing in me.'

'Well, what then? Weren't you winning?'

'I was UK champ three years on the bounce. I won over a million pounds for my owner.'

'Well, what was it then? You can't just give up. Was it bad treatment?'

'Oh, no,' replied the mutt. 'They treated us royally when we were racing.'

'Must have been an injury then?' I guessed.

'Nope. Fit as a flea.'

I was puzzled. 'Then why? I pressed. 'Why did you stop racing?'

'I already told you,' smiled Charlie. 'I quit.'

'You quit?'

'Bingo,' said the dog. 'Simple as that. I quit.'

'But why did you quit?'

'I discovered that what I was chasing was not really a rabbit, and I quit. All that chasing, all that lung-busting running, and what was I chasing? It wasn't even real.'

Charlie put his head back down so that he could be a better pillow for the little boy.

The RISKy business of LOVE

'There is NO safe investment. To LOVE at all is to be vulnerable. LOVE anything, and your ♥ heart ♥ will certainly be wrung and possibly be broken ...'

The Magic Number

The Dunbar number suggests you spend about 40% of your time with between 6 and 8 people. These are your very close family and friends.

Your tribe.

Another big chunk of your time is spent with an additional slightly wider circle of half a dozen.

If we cut to the chase, it boils down to this ...

... you spend about 60% of your entire life with a dozen or so people.

It's worth pausing and thinking about your tribe. Who are your closest dozen?

Because the science is clear. Although you might have 10,000 'friends' online, your well-being is much more likely to be linked to the quality of your relationships with your closest dozen flesh and blood friends and family.

So here's a BIG thought ...

If we aren't careful we can think that we have an infinite amount of time with our loved ones. Let's say your parents are 85, in fine fettle, and expect to get to 95. You see them three times a year. You think that you have 10 more years with them, but you don't.

You have 30 more visits with them!

Are you being the best version of you on those visits? Are you full of love? How are you leaving them feeling at the end of the visit?

Make every visit count!

How do you spell LOVE?

BIG question

Let's start with a truth, and follow up with a problem.

Truth. Every human on the planet wants three things: to be seen, to be heard and to be understood.

Problem. We're getting worse at seeing, hearing and understanding people!

Paradoxically, in our hyper-connected world, more and more people are finding it harder to take the time to simply be with somebody else for a while. We're talking phone in pocket, eye contact, earphones out, with an actual, real person.

Anyone can listen, but to be a black belt communicator you have to be genuinely interested in other people. Yes, *genuinely!*

It's called 'listening with fascination' and it's a fabulous skill to develop. Why? Because most people listen with the intention of *knowing how best to reply*, but when you listen with fascination you do so with the intention of *trying to understand that person better.*[4]

Listening with fascination is about being interested and asking follow-up questions.

Keep your questions positive. So instead of, *'How was your day?'* try subtly rephrasing it to, *'What was the highlight of your day?'* *'What's been the best thing about your day?'* *'What's gone well today?'*

And when they share the good stuff, follow up with the best three words ever - words that will make YOU seem more interesting - which are simply: *'Tell me more ...'*

This page is more important than it looks. Why? Because it reveals the answer to the question:

How do you spell love?

T. I. M. E.

[4]Wondering if you're a good listener? Next time someone's chatting to you, ask yourself this question – am I really listening or just waiting for my turn to speak?

The only really decent thing to do
behind a person's back is to pat it.

The human heart has only four chambers. So
tell me – if we fill it with fear, with hatred,
with doubt and with reservation, where will
we grow our love?

(Bianca Sparacino, author and modern-day philosopher)

Arabic يقبرني (ya'aburnee),

literally, 'you bury me'. This has real depth because it's the hope that a loved one will outlive you so that you will be spared the pain of living life without that person.

Shish, that's big!

Question: How far would you walk to spend time with someone you love?

For info: This is how far the Proclaimers were willing to walk

Iceland

Sweden

Norway

500 Miles

500 More

Ireland

United Kingdom

Poland

Germany

Austria

France

Italy

Spain

Portugal

Word soup

Gigil (Filipino): the urge to squeeze something cute.

Cingulamania (derived from Latin and Greek): the strong desire to hold a person in your arms.

Cafuné (in Brazilian Portuguese) is the act of passionately running fingers through a loved one's hair.

In Korean, the word *jung* means the love in a relationship that is much stronger than romantic love. *Jung* conjures up the feeling of love that will always endure no matter how that love is challenged. I guess we'd call it unconditional.

Cavoli Riscaldati (Italian, literally translated as 'reheated cabbage') is the waste of time spent trying to revive an unworkable relationship. The lesson? If you've tried and tried to make things work, and it still isn't, it's okay to cut your losses.

Global Love

A globetrotting romp through history shows just how far we'll go for LOVE.

In ancient Chinese tradition, it was believed that if you died single your spirit would be lonely and as a result would cause harm to living family members. The obvious solution? Families would arrange 'ghost marriages' between deceased individuals. So, if online dating isn't for you, don't forget a séance is always an option.

Forget the other superfoods; in Aztec culture cacao was believed to be the ultimate aphrodisiac. Legend has it that Montezuma drank gallons of the stuff before visiting his harem. So if you're finding yourself needing a little boost between the sheets, get yourself some bitter, gritty chocolate.

In Medieval Europe, some believed that baking a cake would win you a suitor. Sounds normal enough, except this isn't just any cake. In fact, for the spell to work, the baker would need to strip naked and then rub the dough into their sweaty armpits and, ahem, private parts. Supposedly, once the object of their affection ate a slice, they were destined to fall in love. Nothing says 'I love you' quite like a cake infused with sweat from your pits and bits.

In Finland they have *eukonkanto*. Its origins are a little sketchy, but according to legend (Wikipedia) an outlaw and his band of merry men used to make their living plundering villages and making off with the women. From this ancient barbarism comes *eukonkanto*, aka 'wife carrying', which has now evolved into an annual Wife Carrying Championships. Beamed live on Finnish TV, men carry their wives through an obstacle course with the winner receiving his wife's weight in beer. If your date nights have fallen flat, *eukonkanto* might spice things up.

....

While we have our passports in our hand, let's conclude our global love-in with some different ways to say 'I love you'. These sweet nothings will come in handy whether you're planning a séance, a gallon of hot choc, some naked baking or drinking your spouse's weight in IPA ...

Spanish – Te amo

Polish – Kocham cię

Portuguese – Eu te amo

Swahili – Nakupenda

Turkish – Seni seviyorum

Italian – Ti amo

Indonesian – Aku mencintaimu

German – Ich liebe dich

French – Je t'aime

Finnish – Minä rakastan sinua

Irish – Is tú mo ghrá

Chinese – 我爱你

The sexiest thing you will ever wear is a smile

Here's an interesting way to enhance your levels of loveability – don't be afraid to be a bit of an idiot.

There's something called the *pratfall effect* (honestly, there really is) whereby scientists have proved that you're more attractive if you celebrate your mistakes.

Example. Imagine the party's slacking so you decide to take the bull by the horns and be the first one on the dancefloor.

Nobody follows!

The *pratfall effect* says that rather than retire sheepishly to the bar you should throw whatever shapes you can, with unbridled enthusiasm. No half measures.

The *pratfall effect* (your unashamed silliness) means people will think you're gorgeous.

#PratfallEffect #LoveNotes

Underpant Memories

When mobile phones were invented, the marketing blurb said they were all about giving us freedom.

How's that worked out?

Today most of us are trapped by our smartphones. The real issue is how much they are creeping into our free time. We finish the digital workday and then log onto our digital personal lives

If we are spending all this time on devices, how much time are we missing? How many moments are we not there for because we are sucked into the digital void?

The author, Julia Baird, recalls a time when she was trying to throw out her 10-year-old son's old underpants. His response was, *'But Mum! Think of all the memories in these underpants!'* He was able to regale all the adventures he had while in this particular pair. These underpants held so many memories, they helped him document years of his life.

If he had stayed at home on his device, he would never have had these underpant memories. By being so absorbed in the digital world, we are missing all the underpant memories we could create in the real world.

We all see it: football finals, museums, birthday parties, nativity plays, sunsets, precious family dinners ... we're experiencing them through a screen. Too many people are emotionally and mentally absent from the present moment.

In this busy, chaotic, noisy world we live in, paying attention is honestly the greatest gift you can give.

So do yourself a favour: spend less time on devices and more time with real people. Get out into nature. Unplug. De-stress. Don't let magical moments pass you by.

Go make some underpant memories.

#UnderpantMemories #LoveNotes

The average person looks at their phone `150` times a day.

There's a category of super-users who glance at their beloved screen `358` times a day, and *super*-super-users sneaky-peeking nearly `800` times.

`71%` of people check their phone as soon as they wake up. (`3%` of people sleep with their phone in their hand and `15%` with it under their pillow.)

`64%` of people use their phone on the toilet (and a third of them have dropped their phone down the toilet, some more than once).

`61%` of people have texted someone in the same room as them.

`48%` feel panic or anxiety when their phone battery dips below `20%`.

`36%` would rather give up their pet than their phone.

`66%` of people show signs of nomophobia (smartphone addiction).

`52%` of teenagers sit around in silence, staring at their phones when they are together with friends.

The average phone use is `2` hours and `54` minutes per day (which equals `44` days per year).

The lesson is clear. For eye-to-eye love to blossom, you must break up with your smartphone.

Be careful what sticks

All paint is white. Then they add the tiniest drop of colour, a mere splash of red, blue or yellow and your walls become Butter Biscuit, Antique Map, Amethyst Starling or Raspberry Bellini (yes, these are actual Dulux names).

It's the same with crisps. They're all just fried spuds. Then they stick them in a vat of flavour and they turn into smoky bacon, hedgehog or whatever.

Same with you. You started out as just plain, simple, pure, unadulterated you. Then we stuck you in a big vat of life and flavours stuck to you.

Nobody's born racist. Babies don't hate Mondays. Newborns don't have guilt or jealousy. They don't look at the other babies in the maternity ward and compare: '*Gosh, I've got hamster cheeks. I wish I had normal cheeks like her.*'

We're all born with the capacity to love and learn.

Be careful what sticks.

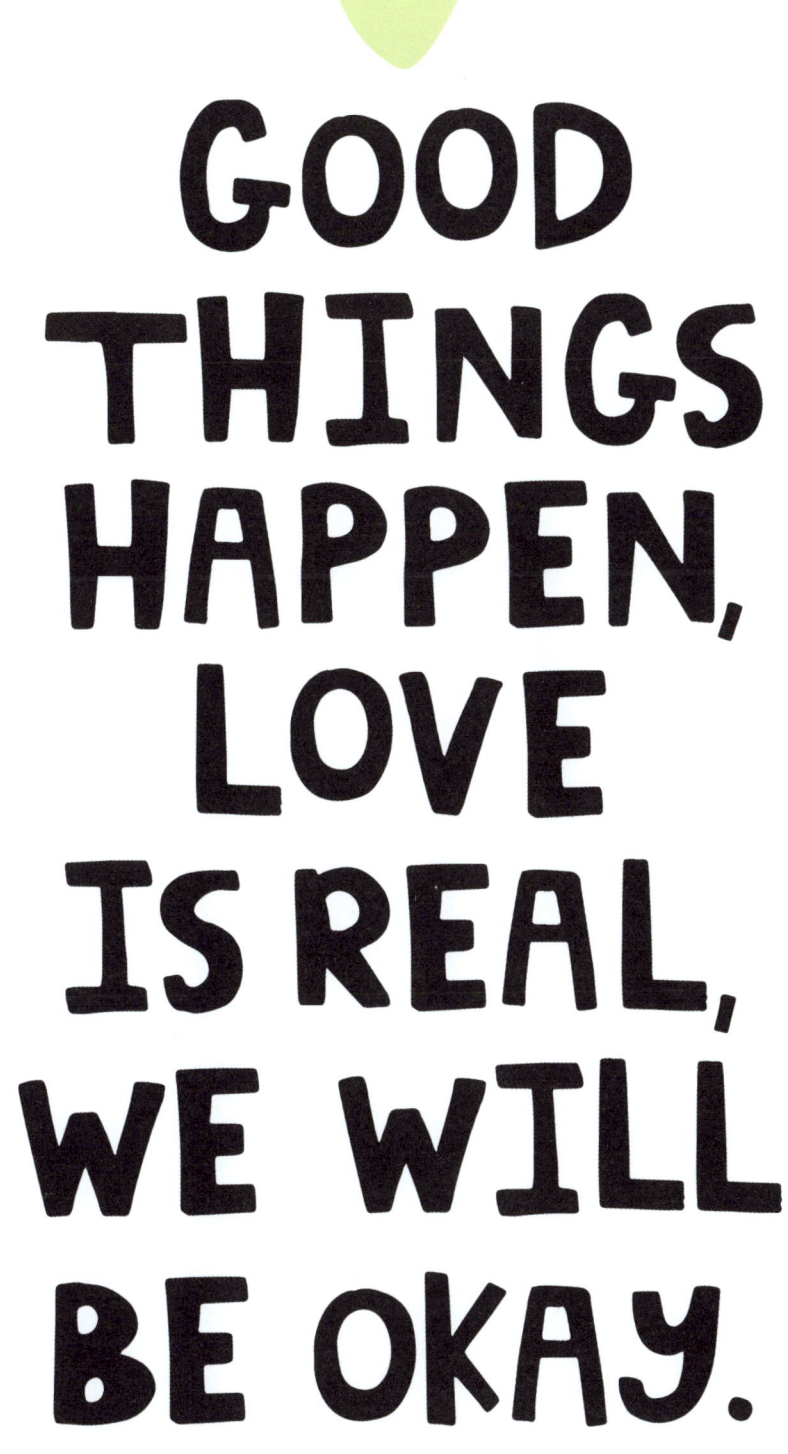

An entirely true LOVE story that we totally made up

In case you don't know (because we didn't!) an allegory is a story with a meaning that you have to work out for yourself.

So no clues from us. The ball of learning is in your court.

Here's the story of Jimmy's diary ...

He hadn't been up there for years. Probably decades! In the faint light of the attic, the old man shuffled across to a pile of boxes that lay near one of the cobwebbed windows. Brushing aside the dust, he began to lift out one old photo album after another.

His search began with the fond recollection of the love of his life — long gone. He knew that somewhere in these albums was the photo he was looking for. It was the black-and-white one, when she had that smile. Patiently opening the long-lost treasures he was soon lost in a sea of memories. The old man wiped away one or two happy tears. Although the world had not stopped spinning when his wife left it, the past was more alive than his present emptiness.

Setting aside one of the dusty albums, he pulled from the box what appeared to be a diary from his son's childhood. He couldn't recall ever having seen it before — or even the fact that his son had kept a diary. Opening the yellowed pages, he glanced over the entries and his lips turned up at the corners in an unconscious smile. His eyes shone and he chuckled aloud. He realised he wasn't just reading the words ... he could hear them, spoken by his young son who'd grown up far too fast in this very house. In the utter silence of the attic, the earnest words of a six-year-old worked their magic and the old man was carried back to a time almost forgotten. The spidery handwriting reflected on important issues for a six-year-old — school, football, holidays, arguments with his big sister — entry after entry stirred a sentimental hunger in the old man's heart. But it was accompanied by a painful memory that his son's simple recollections of those days didn't tally with his own. The old man's wrinkles became more deeply etched.

He remembered that he'd kept a business diary. He closed his son's journal and turned to leave, having forgotten the cherished photo that had triggered his initial search. Hunched over to keep from bumping his head on the beams, the old man stepped down the wooden stairway to his office. He wasn't sure what creaked most, the stairs or his knees!

. He opened a glass cabinet door, reached in and sought his business diary. He placed the journals side by side. His was leather bound, his name embossed in gold. His son's was tatty and frayed with a hand drawn picture on the front. The old man ran a bony finger across the name 'Jimmy' scribbled on the cover.

He opened his business journal and read some of the entries. There were notes from meetings, often very detailed. Every single day was crammed with business appointments. Sometimes the evenings too. He remembered back to those times ... he sure was driven in his career. It was for the love of his family that he'd chased success so hard.

The old man was drawn to an entry much shorter than the rest. In his own neat handwriting were these words, *'Wasted a whole day fishing with Jimmy. Didn't catch a thing!'*

With a deep sigh and a shaking hand he took Jimmy's journal and found the boy's entry for the same day, June 4th. Large scrawling letters pressed deep into the paper read ...

'Went fishing with my dad. Best day of my life.'

(Taken from *The Little Book of Being Brilliant* by Andy Cope)
#JimmysDiary #LoveNotes

Permission to LOVE...

Your LOVE-ability permission slip is valid for the rest of your life and you can use it as often as you want. All you have to do is sign it and remember to use it when you need it.

LOVE-Ability Permission Slip

I hereby grant myself permission to raise my levels of awesomeness. I will not be embarrassed to be stand out amazing. Instead, I will shine and let others catch the glow.

From this day forward, I'm rubber-stamping myself to change what needs changing. I will pat myself on the back when I've earned it, forgive myself when I mess up and allow myself to ask for help when I need it. I give myself licence to let go of negative thinking and habits that might be holding me back.

I'm empowering myself to take life seriously but not take myself too seriously. I authorise myself to raise my personal bar, to go for my dreams, make mistakes and give life a right good run for its money.

I don't need anyone else's approval, *I need mine*. That's why, starting right now, I have the personal stamp of approval to BE myself and to LIKE myself. Not in an over-the-top sickly self-love way, but in a quietly confident 'I've got this' way.

My LOVE-ability starts with me but extends outwards. I hereby grant myself permission to LOVE and to be loved. This love extends to people (EVEN THE ANNOYING ONES), all living things (INCLUDING SPIDERS) and to life itself.

Ashes to ashes.

Dust to dust.

Funk to funky.

Till death do I part.

Because I'm worth it.

Love,

Your signature

Date

'Looking BACK over a lifetime, YOU see that LOVE was the answer to EVERYTHING'

(Ray Bradbury, author and screenwriter)

Hiraeth
(Welsh):

A deeply felt
connection to
one's homeland.

(side effect:
causes singing
in the valleys)

The real TiK ToK.
Time is precious,
don't waste it.

The Love Test

Here's the sure-fire way to find out who loves you more, your partner or your dog.

Lock them both in the boot of your car for three hours. When you pop the boot open, see which one's most pleased to see you.

#BeMoreDog #LoveNotes

DOG'S DIARY

BESTday of my life	**BEST**day of my life	**BEST**day of my life	**BEST**day of my life	**BEST**day of my life
BESTday of my life	**BEST**day of my life	**BEST**day of my life	**BEST**day of my life	**BEST**day of my life
BESTday of my life	**BEST**day of my life	**BEST**day of my life	**BEST**day of my life	**BEST**day of my life
BESTday of my life	**BEST**day of my life	**BEST**day of my life	**BEST**day of my life	**BEST**day of my life
BESTday of my life	**BEST**day of my life	**BEST**day of my life	**BEST**day of my life	**BEST**day of my life
BESTday of my life	**BEST**day of my life	**BEST**day of my life	**BEST**day of my life	**BEST**day of my life
BESTday of my life	**BEST**day of my life	**BEST**day of my life	**BEST**day of my life	**BEST**day of my life
BESTday of my life	**BEST**day of my life	**BEST**day of my life	**BEST**day of my life	**BEST**day of my life
BESTday of my life	**BEST**day of my life	**BEST**day of my life	**BEST**day of my life	**BEST**day of my life

Creating a LOVE ripple

Sometimes you'll walk into a room and sense an empathy vacuum. Fill it with love, compassion, enthusiasm and listening.

While it's true that we cannot force people to be positive, we can plant seeds. It is truly a case of leading by example. Your attitudes and behaviours are infectious. I guess the million-dollar double-barrelled question is: who will you 'emotionally infect' and what will you 'infect' them with?

A research paper reports that a happy friend makes you 25% happier (but only if they live within a mile of you), a happy brother or sister raises your happiness by 14% and a happy neighbour raises your happiness by a whopping 34%.

It boils down to this. Humans are wired to catch each other's emotions. You cannot NOT have an impact.

If you can't be bothered to be happy for yourself, cultivate it for those closest to you.

Be that friend.
Be that sibling.
Be that neighbour.

BREAKING NEWS...

If you watch the news it's easy to think that happiness and kindness are in short supply. The world's reserves of LOVE seem to be running dangerously low.

It's fake news people!

Remember what the news actually is – *deviations from the norm.*

Intrepid reporters are curators of misery. They seek out hotspots of trauma, disaster, crime, murder, famine, poverty, catastrophe, corruption, failure and tragedy. They pick out the world's most despicable acts of hate, unhappiness and unkindness and beam them directly onto your eyeballs.

'Neighbour makes an extra meal and takes it to the old man living next door' does not make the News at 10.

'Son returns home from uni and gets huge hug off his mum' fails to register on the disaster-ometer.

'Married couple still in love after 30 years' is heart-warming, but not newsworthy.

There is no intrepid hack babbling excitedly, *'This teenager has just let this elderly lady go in front of him in the supermarket queue.'*

Here's a headline you'll never see: *'Breaking news: the vast majority of people slept safely in their comfy beds last night. They were warm, well fed and not at war.'*

Here's the news-grabbing headline: *'Billions of small acts of happiness, kindness and love go unreported every single day.'*

That, dear reader, is a scandal.

Good old days

Fast-forward to when you're 102. Imagine you're sitting in your care home, slumped in your chair, a nice carer spooning soup into your mouth. She's hugely encouraging, but it's a messy business.

Dare to put yourself in that situation and reflect on your life.

You'll reminisce on days gone by when you had fine health, a quick mind, could walk unaided and were capable of eating soup all on your own.

Go you!

Ahhh, the good old days.

The chances are that today – and yesterday, and tomorrow, and last year, and next year – these are the good old days.

So it makes sense to quit waiting. Rather than waiting until age 102 to enjoy the good old days, why not LOVE today, *today?*

#GoodOldDays #LoveNotes

Be the LIGHT

It's a fact that bad things happen to good people.

There are times when those closest to you will struggle.

Remember, the light at the end of their tunnel could be you.

Primed for LOVE

Airport security can be a little undignified. You're often required to step into a glass chamber, legs splayed, arms aloft, as they take some sort of naked picture of you.

We don't question it.

We do as they ask, hanging onto the glimmer of positivity that the naked picture shows your back passage is clear of heroin, and as degrading as the system is, it's more humane than the alternative rubber-glove treatment.

This heightened security has spread to concerts and public gatherings. There's a wonderful story about Kai, a four-year-old boy who was new to all this. A keen WWE wrestling fan, his dad took him to a big venue where fans were routinely frisked on entry.

All of them, even the four-year-olds!

The boy wandered through the metal detector, the red light picking out the £2 spending money buried in his pocket. The security guard knelt down to the boy's level and opened his arms, showing the four-year-old what was required. The lad, assuming the best, opened his arms and went in for the full hug.

And that was where the newspaper story ended. Whether security went on to discover a flick-knife tucked into the lad's belt, or a kilo of hash in his socks, who knows?

I'd say it's unlikely because Kai is how we all start out, primed for LOVE, not hate.

It's a parenting thing ...

Absolutely true ...

Rewind to the start of the 20th century. The prevailing parenting wisdom was that hugging and kissing your children would spread germs, while letting them sit on your lap, holding hands and all that bedtime story nonsense would make them weak of character. Too much love was a dangerous thing.

At around the same time, we started to understand about germs and, in a massive breakthrough for patient safety, medical staff were scrubbed up and hospital floors polished until they shone.

These super-hygienic, no hugging, 'speak when you're spoken to' environments were also applied to orphanages. Remember, this was the 1900s. It was common for your mum and dad to have expired well before 30 or that they couldn't afford to feed you, so you were wrapped in swaddling clothes and deposited on an orphanage doorstep.

Digging around in history, you find the orphanage mortality rate was close to 100%. Yes, you read that correctly. In some orphanages, *almost every single child died before they were two years old.*

The dorms were completely sterile, the tiles were scrubbed to shining, each infant's bed was a safe distance from the next, and each crib covered with mosquito netting. Each baby was touched only when absolutely necessary, which was hardly ever. It was a quick nappy change, a feed, and then back in your sterilised crib for 23 hours.

The noble aim of preventing the spread of germs meant that the children were dying from lack of love.

Cutting to the chase, people need people. This is important at all ages but especially so in the early years.

So get off your phone and into your children's lives.

Let me say it again, but this time imagine I'm kneeling at your feet, hands clasped, looking up at you and pleading with every fibre of my being: *please get off your phone and into your children's lives.*

Love your children, even when they haven't earned it. Hold their little hand in yours. Read the best bedtime stories. Snuggle. Laugh. Be silly. Kiss. Rub noses. Build dens. Blow raspberries on their tummies, yes, even when they're 19.

In times when you haven't really got time, *make some.*

It starts with kids but it's not just about kids.

All the people in your life, young and old alike, need more than food and shelter to live full and healthy lives.

They need love, hugs and human touch.

Oodles and oodles of it.

GREET your CHILD with a SMILE, NOT a MOBILE.

The Matthew Effect

The little known but oh-so-powerful 'Matthew Effect' is when an initial success in something leads to even greater success. And conversely, if we are unsuccessful we're likely to become even more unsuccessful.

Let's take the example of reading – children who start off reading well will get better and better compared to their peers because they will read even more broadly and quickly. The more words they learn the easier and more enjoyable reading becomes.

On the other hand, it's very hard for poor readers to catch up because for them the spiral goes downwards. Thus the gap between those who read well and those who read poorly grows even bigger rather than smaller.

According to the Matthew Effect, success snowballs, but so does failure.

The Matthew Effect shows up everywhere. If you want your children to find their passion (sport, maths, cooking, science, stand-up comedy; it doesn't matter what) the Matthew Effect says that some early wins are crucial in your child powering ahead.

The biggest thing you can do to facilitate whatever they love to do is to put yourself out there. If you child is learning the violin, challenge yourself to learn it too.

Play together. Paint together. Laugh together.

Trampolining. Bounce together.

Baking. Make cakes together.

Art. Draw together.

Stand-up comedy. Tell jokes together.

Science. Dissect frogs together.

Football. Kick about together.

Spellings. Learn them together.

Drama. Go to the theatre together.

#LoveTogether #MatthewEffect #LoveNotes

Terminal!

Here's a true story, which makes it all the more compelling.

A doctor decided to ask her patients what they enjoyed in life and what gave it meaning. All well and good, except this doctor happened to work with terminally ill children.

'Terminal' is just the worst word. In an airport a terminal is where your journey ends and in a children's hospice that journey is life. They're not going to get to experience the pleasures of being an adult and their parents aren't going to enjoy the joys of parenting.

Gulp!

Here are some of the children's responses.

First: none said they wished they'd watched more TV, zero said they wished they'd spent more time on Facebook, zilch said they enjoyed fighting with others and not one of them enjoyed hospital.

Interestingly, lots mentioned their pets and almost all mentioned their parents, often expressing worry or concern such as, *'I hope mum will be okay. She seems sad,'* and *'Dad mustn't worry. He'll see me again one day in heaven maybe.'*

Double gulp!

All of them loved ice-cream. *Fact!*

Also, they all loved books or being told stories, especially by their parents.

Many wished they had spent less time worrying about what others thought of them and valued people who just treated them 'normally'. For example, *'My real friends didn't care when my hair fell out.'*

Many of them loved swimming and the beach. Almost all of them valued kindness above most other virtues.

All of them loved people who made them laugh: *'The boy in the next bed farted! Hahaha!'* (Laughter relieves pain.)

And finally, they ALL valued time with their family. Nothing was more important. *'Mum and dad are the best!' 'My sister always hugs me tight' 'No one loves me like mummy loves me!'*

Triple gulp!

Look here, dear reader, these are very big messages indeed. If you can't be bothered to listen to anything else in this book, then please listen to children who are arriving at the final destination of their very short lives.

If we're allowed to summarise, it'd be something like this: Be kind. Read more bedtime stories (and read them like you want to), spend time with your family, crack jokes, lighten up, fart in bed, go to the beach, hug your kids.

Love, love and more love.

Oh ... and eat ice-cream. Often.

Hang on tight ...

Love is what
makes the ride
worthwhile.

'Where there is LOVE, there is life☺.'

(Gandhi. A humble figure.
Giant of change.)

Never put a skunk on a bus

Here are a few nuggets of wisdom about LOVE and LIFE, from the mouths of babes ...

'You gotta say your affirmations in your mouth and your heart. You say, 'I am brave for this meeting!', 'I am loved!', 'I smell good!' And you can say five or three or ten until you know it.'

Isaak, age 6

'Never put a skunk on a bus.'

Milo, age 5

'Think about the donuts of your day! Even if you cry a little, you can think about potato crisps!'

Tommy, age 7

'You gotta take a deep breath and you gotta do it again.'

Abi, age 8

'Even if it's a yucky day, you can get a hug.'

Femi, age 4

'When your mum is mad at your dad, don't let her brush your hair.'

Talyia, age 11

'When someone loves you, the way they say your name is different. You just know that your name is safe in their mouth.'

Billy, age 4

'Love is when you go out to eat and give somebody most of your French fries without making them give you any of theirs.'

Chrissie, age 6

'Love is what makes you smile when you're tired.'

Terri, age 4

'Monsters are less scary when they're peeing.'

Tommy, age 6

'Love is when your puppy licks your face even after you've left him alone all day.'

Mary Ann, age 4

Lulu reminded Henry, 'Before we make love could you put out the bins?'

Negative capability

John Keats penned some poetic masterpieces but it's a phrase he wrote in a letter to his brothers in 1817 that might just be the most useful definition of love ever: negative capability.

Let me explain ...

Keats described negative capability as the ability to have two different ideas in your head at the same time. This is super useful because love is full of contradictions, messiness and mixed messages.

For example, mild irritation can sit alongside love. Even though your partner might be driving you mad saying the cushions need to be placed in a certain way, you still adore them.

In the same vein, imperfection can sit alongside lust. Oh, those muffin tops!

Negative capability is also useful for those moments when you say one thing but mean another. For example:

'I'm fine.'

Actual meaning: *'I am absolutely not fine and yes, it is your fault.'*

'Have you emptied the bin?'

Actual meaning: *'I know you haven't emptied the bin. I am giving you one last chance to redeem yourself.'*

'Let's watch something we both like.'

Actual meaning: *'We are going to watch something I like.'*

'I don't mind where we eat.'

Actual meaning: *'I really do mind where we eat and if you really loved me, you would know the answer.'*

Negative capability means you don't have to attend every argument you're invited to. Used wisely it saves you from spontaneously combusting, bickering, silent treatment or getting divorced.

ORDINARY
MAGIC

Ordinary MAGIC

These last few years, it's almost as if civilisation has become less ... *civil?*

They say that what doesn't break ~~you makes you stronger which, like~~ all sayings, is mostly true. It doesn't apply to bears. For the record, bears will rip you apart with their sharp claws.

But we get the wider point: you grow stronger through adversity.

Love brings joy, but also despair. People fall in love and then sometimes one of them falls out of love.

A heart breaks.

Human beings are equipped with 'ordinary magic'. This special elixir, sometimes called 'time', heals almost anything.

When your heart is in a zillion pieces, you question everything, especially yourself. When your head is screaming that you can't ever love again, your ordinary magic says you can ...

Eventually.

The process of recovery can begin one small step at a time.

It's actually quite heroic. Ordinary magic is about hanging in there during the worst of times.

Dig deep. Give your 'ordinary magic' some time to kick in.

Should you love things and use people,
or love people and use things?

It's your call.

Children who are born into happy families grow up speaking love, kindness and positivity as their native language.

#Fact

A l o h a !

No description of love would be complete without the Hawaiian word *aloha.*

There's a lot crammed into those five letters!

Alo is about 'sharing, in the present',

Oha means 'joyous affection',

and *Ha* is 'breath'.

Aloha packs quite a punch.

The Hawaiian islanders use it to encompass peace, love, compassion, grace, charity, sympathy, gentle sharing, hello, good-bye and much more.

Aloha is a classic example of a word that cannot be translated simply using one word.

Aloha is a philosophy to live and love by.

The 'yes-no' game of LOVE

That pesky 'yes' word!

We are all so guilty of saying 'yes' to things we don't want to do. But 'yes' comes at a price. When you say 'yes' to something you *don't* want to do, you're saying 'no' to something you *do* want to do!

Permission to say 'NO!'

We need to learn to give ourselves permission to use the 'no' word, because 'no' is empowering. Saying 'no' to things frees us up to do what is most important, what invigorates us, what energises us and what makes us feel alive.

But 'yes' is easy, and 'no' is hard!

True story ...

Once upon a time there was a 12-year-old girl who loved her dad but didn't see much of him. He was a keynote speaker with a super-busy diary and tens of thousands of motorway miles on the clock.

Which is why she was so excited to have a daddy-daughter night out scheduled. She was sooooo looking forward to a simple evening, a pizza or burger, and definitely a milkshake, just her and her dad.

They had been planning it for months. He was doing a talk in his hometown, so as soon as her dad had finished his presentation, she joined in the applause, jumped up from her seat, and slipped her hand into his.

But before she could steal him away, her father was approached by an old friend who he'd not seen in ages. There was back-slapping and laughter, and the friend invited them to have an incredible dinner at a jaw-dropping restaurant. The little girl didn't know anything about Michelin stars or maître d's, but apparently this place had both!

The 12-year-old was crestfallen. She was sure lobster thermidor would be perfectly nice, but her heart was set on a cheeseburger. She didn't want to go to a fancy restaurant. She didn't want to hear more about business. She didn't want to share her dad with an old friend and whoever Dom Perignon was. She wanted a simple night, just the two of them, being a little bit silly.

But suddenly her dad turned to his old friend and said that, despite it all sounding fantastic, he had other plans and, unfortunately, they couldn't be changed. In hindsight, it was a really polite 'NO'.

He took his little girl by the hand and went on to have the night they had been planning for months.

Years later, she still talks about that particular evening and how that simple act of her dad saying 'no' to his friend meant he said 'YES' to her.

It was a bond. She knew that she mattered. The little girl knew that she was loved. That little girl's father was Stephen R. Covey, who wrote *The Seven Habits of Highly Effective People*, and one of his principles was: *the main thing is to keep the main thing the main thing.*

The moral of the story: learn to say 'no', so you can say 'yes' to what *really* matters.

How are you supposed to LOVE the darkest and MOST flawed parts of the person your heart chooses, if you won't allow yourself to LOVE your own?

(SORRY, that's proper deep. We should have given a BIG MEANINGFUL SENTENCE alert.)

'All we are is peace, love and wisdom, and the power to create the illusion that we're not'

(Jack Pransky, American author and Speaker)

LOVE the seasons

I love summer in the UK. It's my favourite day of the year.

Which brings us onto the weather! About 50% of conversations start with the weather. It's an easy way in, usually by means of a low-level grumble about it being too hot, cold, windy, rainy, snowy, dry, grey, foggy, humid, blustery, misty, wet, dark, hurricaney ... and just occasionally, *lovely!*

So it pays to learn to LOVE whatever the seasons throw at us, which, plot spoiler, is likely to be a lot!

To get your conversation starter muscles tuned to positive, have an argument with yourself about the seasons.

Here are your 4 argument starters:

1. Spring takes a bit of beating. It's totally and *literally* lush! Spring is definitely the best season because ...

2. No way! There's literally no point having a debate. Everyone knows summer is the best. Here's what's epic about the summer season ...

3. Autumn is the unsung hero of the seasons. Look around. Soak it up. It's absolutely 110% the best time of year because ...

4. Don't you just love winter? I mean, what an utterly fabulous time of year. Here's why it's my all-time fave season ...

When you like a flower, you pick it.

When you love a flower, you water it.

Make of it what you will but maybe it's about ditching the short cuts, the life hacks and the pursuit of shiny things. It's about taking time and effort to invest in people and to nurture relationships, including you with yourself.

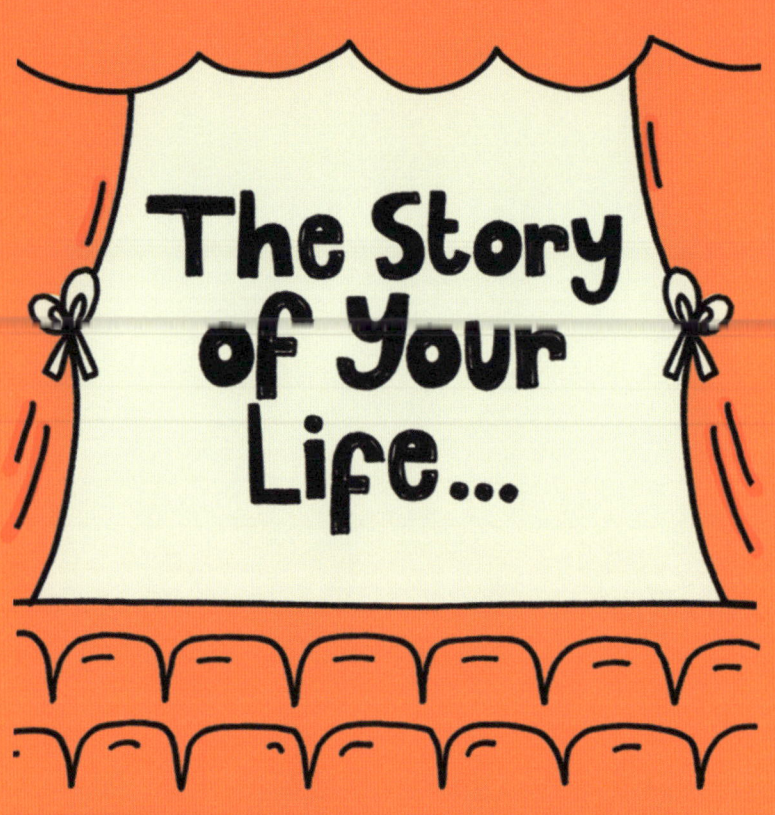

The Story of Your Life...

If you're to fall in love with life you have to embrace the *whole* show: the laughing, crying, terrifying, angry, happy, sad, joyous, embarrassing, boring, regrettable bits ...
Because this is your life!

If we told you it's impossible
to lick your elbow, you're
gonna have to give it a try.

If we said you can insert 'only'
anywhere in this next sentence,
you're gonna have to give it a
try ...

She told him that she loved him.

Love your imperfections

We understand the pressures. We really do. The mantras of 'being your best self' and 'living your best life' have been insidiously drip-fed into us since, well ... *forever.*

But the truth is that nobody feels amazing all the time (except your dog, right?)

And here's a dirty little secret: all those who claim to be living their best life ... they've got the same insecurities and fears as you and I.

There's a technical term for it. It's called BEING HUMAN!

So, yes, in the real world you'll have your bad days that will often be accompanied by negative thoughts and behaviours. You're still amazing though. Just not perfect.

The Japanese have a word for it: *wabi-sabi.* This wonderful concept is founded on three simple realities: nothing lasts, nothing is finished and nothing is perfect.

Wabi-sabi is the essence of being perfectly imperfect.

It's often applied to art and pottery. So, for example, drinking your hot chocolate from your favourite mug is *wabi-sabi.* Not only are you comfortable with the fact that your go-to mug is simple, rustic and chipped, but its lack of class also somehow adds to your drinking pleasure.

You like it *because* it's chipped! Take away the imperfection and you take away the charm, you take away what makes it special.

You've got your favourite wabi-sabi jumper for slobbing around the house. It's baggy and old, but you love it.

You've got a wabi-sabi cuddly toy that's been hugged almost to death. It's got a bald patch and lost an eye – but you don't love it any less!

The Japanese don't generally apply the principle to people, but they're missing a trick. *Wabi-sabi* maps across effortlessly.

Remember, nothing lasts, nothing is finished and nothing is perfect. Including all eight billion of us.

That means your quirks, anomalies and imperfections are the most beautiful things in the world. Your lack of class is somehow classy!

That mole on your chin, that slightly crooked nose, your wonky feet, those few straggly strands of hair that refuse to behave, those wrinkles around your eyes, your shyness, your muffin tops, the way you blush, the fact you can't take a compliment, your gappy teeth, you could do with being a couple of inches taller – or shorter – the sleep in your eye, your scruffy jeans, your insecurities, your saggy bits, your fear of spiders, your terrible parking, your snoring, your coffee breath, the fact that you'd prefer to stay in than go to the party, the fact you're still smarting from a comment a teacher made all those years ago ...

... your foibles. Your blemishes. Your YOU-niqueness.

I am most definitely *wabi-sabi*. You are *wabi-sabi*. Everyone is *wabi-sabi*. We're all human beings, beautifully crafted by wear and tear.

You are flawed beauty.

Revel in your imperfections. Why? Because they make you, you.

Oh, and it helps if you understand that nobody else really cares about your imperfections. Often, they haven't even noticed your faults because they're so busy worrying about their own.

Gosh, you're beautiful!

#wabisabi #LoveNotes

The most
LOVING
people I know:

1. Go out in all weathers
2. Live in the moment
3. Are full of enthusiasm for life
4. Love a good walk
5. Are totally loyal
6. Are not on social media
7. Are not actually people
8. Are dogs

woof

#BeMoreDog #Woof

Sitting comfortably?

Finland is currently sitting at #1 in the international league tables of happiness, so there must be something we can learn from the Finns?

Indeed there is ...

Hyppytyynytyydytys, a vowelless mouthful which translates as 'your favourite bounciest cushion'. Imagine, having an actual word for the feeling of plonking your backside onto your favourite cushion?

No wonder they're so happy!

Important numbers:

9: number of lives, if you're a cat. Warning, humans generally get fewer.

43,252,003,274,489,856,000: the total number of configurations on a Rubik's Cube.

101: the room in which George Orwell put his worst nightmares.

7: the world's favourite lucky number.

13: not so lucky.

42: the meaning of life (according to Hitchhikers the galaxy over).

18: almost but not quite grown up. Ditto **21.** Also **40, 57** and **106.**

50: the number of ways to leave your lover, according to Paul Simon.

3: according to our lazy Google search, this is the number of times we can fall in proper love. And guess what, each serves a purpose:

a) First love. Normally overwhelms you in your teenage years. We tend to believe that our first love will be our last, our one and only, and sometimes it is.

b) Second love. Sometimes called 'hard love', it teaches us lessons about ourselves and can bring the pain of deceit and loss. We can get stuck in a 'second love loop' where we believe that with this person it'll be different, but in reality … it's the same old disappointing result. Too many people make do at the hard love stage.

c) Third love. The love that NO ONE expects … the love that will surprise you because it lands when you're not looking. This love is considered to be the 'easy love' – the love that is simple with no complications. It's not the love you dreamed of, but it's pretty damned good.

Oh, and there's one more super-important number …

Number 1: someone you should really look after.

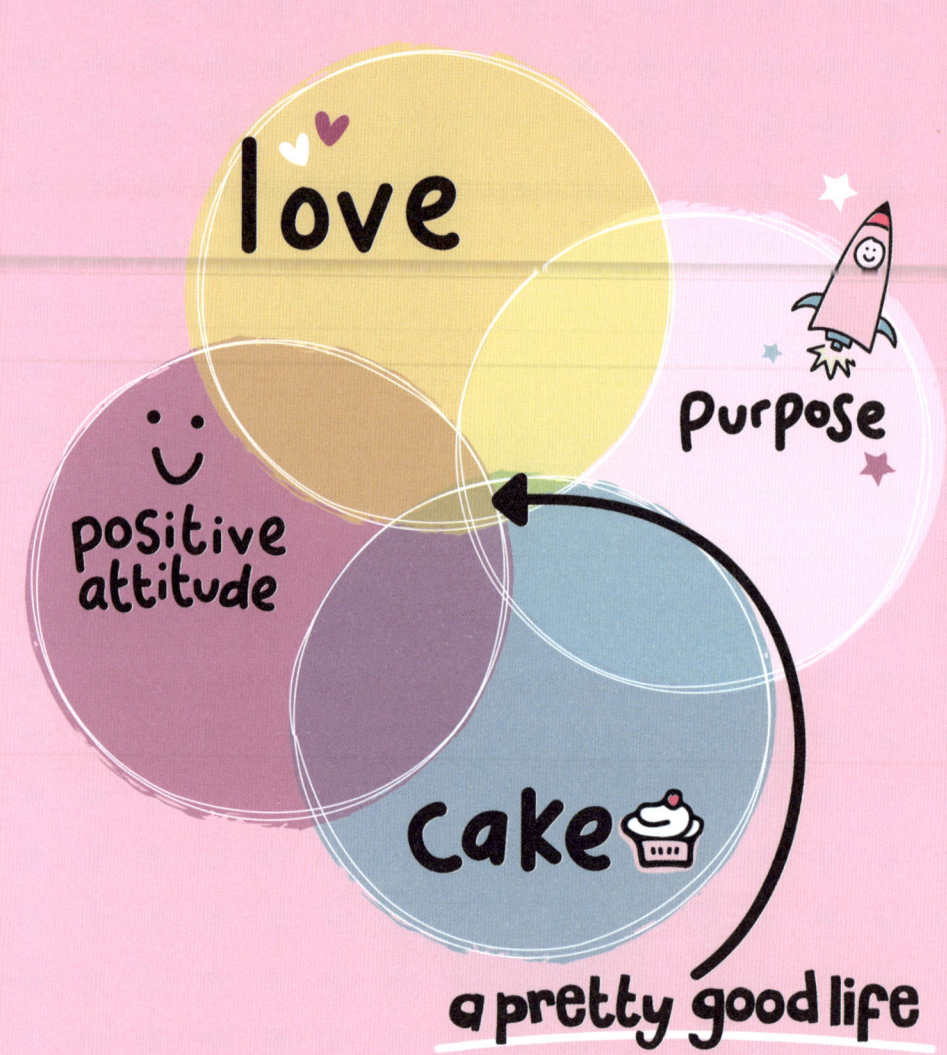

love

purpose

positive
attitude

cake

a pretty good life

Probably true ...

The warmth of your heart prevents your body from rusting.

Why it's always now or never

All the way from Japan we bring you the sublime beauty of *ichi-go ichi-e*, literally translated as 'for this time only' and also as 'in this moment, an opportunity'.

Originating from 16th century tea ceremonies, *ichi-go ichi-e* recognises that every moment we experience is a unique treasure that will never be repeated in the same way again. So, for example, on the surface, a cup of tea with your family might seem like an everyday occasion but each gathering is a unique experience. The exact same people having a cup of tea tomorrow will create a different atmosphere.

That means family moments that happen every day are all special. Each gathering is unique. So if we let them slip away without enjoying them, the moment will be lost forever.

Becoming aware of *ichi-go ichi-e* helps you take your foot off the accelerator and remember that each moment you spend in the world, every moment you spend with your family, is infinitely valuable and deserves your full attention.

Each opportunity presents itself only once. If you don't embrace it, it's lost forever. It really is a case of life being now or never.

It's about regressing back to being a hunter-gatherer – not of wild pigs and berries, but of moments. *This* breakfast, *this* bedtime story, *this* walk, *this* trip to the supermarket, *this* time the cat sits on your knee, *this* frosty morning, this hug, *this* bowl of washing up, *this* chat with your daughter, *this* walk in the drizzle …

Awareness of *ichi-go ichi-e* means you feel much less weighed down by the past or anxious about the future. It's a super-clever form of mindfulness that leaves you smiling inside.

Embrace *ichi-go ichi-e* because life is too short to be busy.

146

LOVE conquers all

Winston Churchill wasn't perfect, but he crammed some BIG achievements into a single lifetime.

His biggest, according to Winston himself ...

'My MOST brilliant achievement was my ability to be able to persuade my wife to MARRY me'

It's NOW o'clock...

My gran had a special Crown Derby tea set that was on display in a glass cabinet in her kitchen. It was used on special occasions and for special visitors, which was pretty much almost exactly *never*.

Day to day, we all drank from chipped mugs.

Hatch, match and dispatch. Basically, the three records inked into the world database are your birth, marriage and death certificates.

Inevitably, my gran reached the 'dispatch' phase. With one of the most fabulous women in the world gone, the extended family and a bunch of hangers-on did what you do. We trudged back from the church to gran's house where there would be sandwiches, cakes and tea.

My grandma would have been pleased to know that her death was deemed an occasion special enough for us all to be sipping milky tea from her very best Crown Derby bone china collection.

Oh, the irony. The tea set she'd spent a lifetime not using was being filled and refilled at her own funeral. I reflected on my pristine cup, saucer and matching plate and couldn't help thinking I wish they'd been chipped and cracked and used every single day.

Saving your best for a special occasion takes on a different meaning when you understand that life is the ultimate special occasion.

No, scrub that. NOW is the ultimate special occasion.

#NOWoclock #LoveNotes

The two most important days of your life?

Hazard your best guess? The most important days of your ENTIRE life ...

(Correct answers are on the final page.)

Filthy rich?

There's a strong chance that you already have riches beyond your wildest dreams. One of the London universities has worked this out:

- Having good friends and relatives is worth £64,000 a year to you
- Having nice neighbours is worth £37,000 a year
- And the biggy, excellent health is estimated to be worth £300,000 a year to you

We sincerely hope you can tick some of the boxes above. So here's another very big point. We take the things above for granted. We fail to spot them and our attention is focused on all the stuff we *haven't* got.

Taking the argument to the extreme, I guess you could trade in your family, friends, neighbours and good health and collect about £400,000. And we're sure you'd be nearly half a million pounds richer but so much poorer.

My goal is to be filthy rich.
Rich in knowledge.
Rich in adventure.
Rich in laughter
Rich in health.
Rich in family.
Rich in love.

'Everyone thinks of changing the world, but no
one thinks of changing himself.'

Leo Tolstoy, author

Some do, Mr. Tolstoy. I promise you.
Some *really* do.

For Daisy

I remember the first day we brought our daughter home from the hospital. Both sides of the family were waiting, not so patiently, to meet her. It was like the opening scene of *The Lion King*, when Simba is lifted up to be shown off to the animal kingdom.

As Daisy was passed between her grandparents, they all cooed, fell immediately in love with their new granddaughter and remarked how small she was, how wrinkly she was, how cute she was, what an amazing head of hair and repertoire of funny faces she had.

And all four mused about the kind of person she might turn out to be. She was just one day old and the old folks were already trying to predict her future!

Daisy's birth followed an incredible summer of sport so athleticism was clearly on everyone's mind. Will she be the next elite gymnast? Britain's next heptathlete? A rower, runner or a Lioness?

I remember looking down at my daughter as I held her in my arms, this tiny ball of human potential doing her best Kenneth Williams impression. She could be anything. The world is her oyster. Sure, I would be delighted if she became an Olympian or helped England win a World Cup.

But there's something much bigger than that.

I vowed to support her in whatever path she chooses, but all I thought as I held her close, the thing I wanted most for my daughter was for her to always know that she is loved.

I love you with my whole heart

Cloud 9

When life gets complicated, I always calm myself with Charles Horton Cooley's soothingly simple message: *'I am not what I think I am and I am not what you think I am. I am what I think that you think I am.'*

With that cleared up let's move to love, with depth. And height. Let me explain ...

LIFE is the only game where the objective seems to be to work out the rules.

It's easy to live a *coulda, shoulda, woulda* life of *if onlys* ...

And then all too soon, just when you think you've figured out how to play the game, your time's up. Nobody truly knows where you go when you die but for the sake of this page please humour us and assume that we emigrate up there. Let's call it 'the cloud' or 'cloud 9'.

In which case it's worth thinking about those who are already there. You might have loved ones who've passed away. Imagine them sitting on cloud 9, looking down on us as we go about our day to day. Remember, these are the people who've had their time. They've lived their lives.

They know all about *coulda, shoulda, woulda.*

They've experienced their own personal *if onlys* ...

And they love you, which means they're rooting for you.

Let's get silly and play around with what they're absolutely *not* saying. They're unlikely to be advising you to play small. Your heavenly cheerleaders aren't yelling for you to take no risks or shy away from opportunities or challenges. They're not urging you to spend more time scrolling on your phone or watching reality TV. They're not recommending that you carry a mediocre attitude around with you. They're not bellowing, 'Frown, baby, frown.' They're not recommending that you slouch around and only come alive at weekends. They're not demanding that you should be full of self-doubt and that you should be cautious in love in case you get your heart broken.

The heavenly refugees have had their chance and they want you to make the most of yours! They're up there, screaming at you to go for it! Seize every single day! Take some calculated risks and go for opportunities when they show up. I can hear them screaming, *'If there aren't any opportunities, create some!'* Get off your phone and look up, the world's amazing. Make eye contact with life. Smile. Be confident. Create friendships. Quit coasting. Lose the excuses. Craft an attitude that makes people go wow. Get out of bed an hour earlier than everyone else and work on your secret long-term ambition. Eat the right foods, drink gallons of H_2O, get good-quality sleep. It's okay to mess up. It doesn't matter if you sometimes fail or look silly. In fact, failure makes you stronger and remember the pratfall effect from earlier? Looking a bit silly is kind of sexy.

We 100% guarantee your heavenly champions are yelling for you to believe in yourself and squeeze the maximum value out of *every single moment* of *every single day.*

As for love, those up there know the truth ... those who risk nothing are, in actual fact, risking everything! Love starts very close to home. It has to start with the person in the mirror. No, not sickly self-love but genuine admiration and respect for the person reflected back at you.

Because how can you expect anyone else to love you if you can't be bothered to love yourself?

Those cloud dwellers are desperate for you to make the most of your time down there because, hey, one day it'll be your turn to emigrate to cloud 9.

Until that day comes, commit to no more *if onlys.* Banish the *coulda, shoulda, woulda* mindset.

I dream of good news.

One day I hope to wake up to the BBC headline proclaiming, 'Peace, love and friendship have been declared throughout the world.'

I'm ever hopeful, but not holding my breath.

Meantime, all I can do is BE peace, love and friendship.

The planet
desperately needs
more peacemakers,
healers and lovers
of all kinds.

'To have been LOVED so deeply, even though the person who LOVED us is gone, will give us some protection FOREVER'

(Albus Dumbledore, Wizard)

PUBLIC HEALTH
WARNING

Don't delete your mental health. Delete your apps!

Sixteenth-century fact

Most people got married in June because they took their yearly bath in May and still smelled pretty good by June. However, since they were starting to smell, brides carried a bouquet of flowers to hide the body odour. Hence the custom today of carrying a bouquet when getting married.

Shortest poem ever written:

'Me.
We'.

(Muhammed Ali, pugilist)

Imagine if WE ALL carried an attitude of unconditional LOVE for our fellow humans. And picture humanity if we all wore a smile and walked with a spring in our step ... Who knows what might happen?

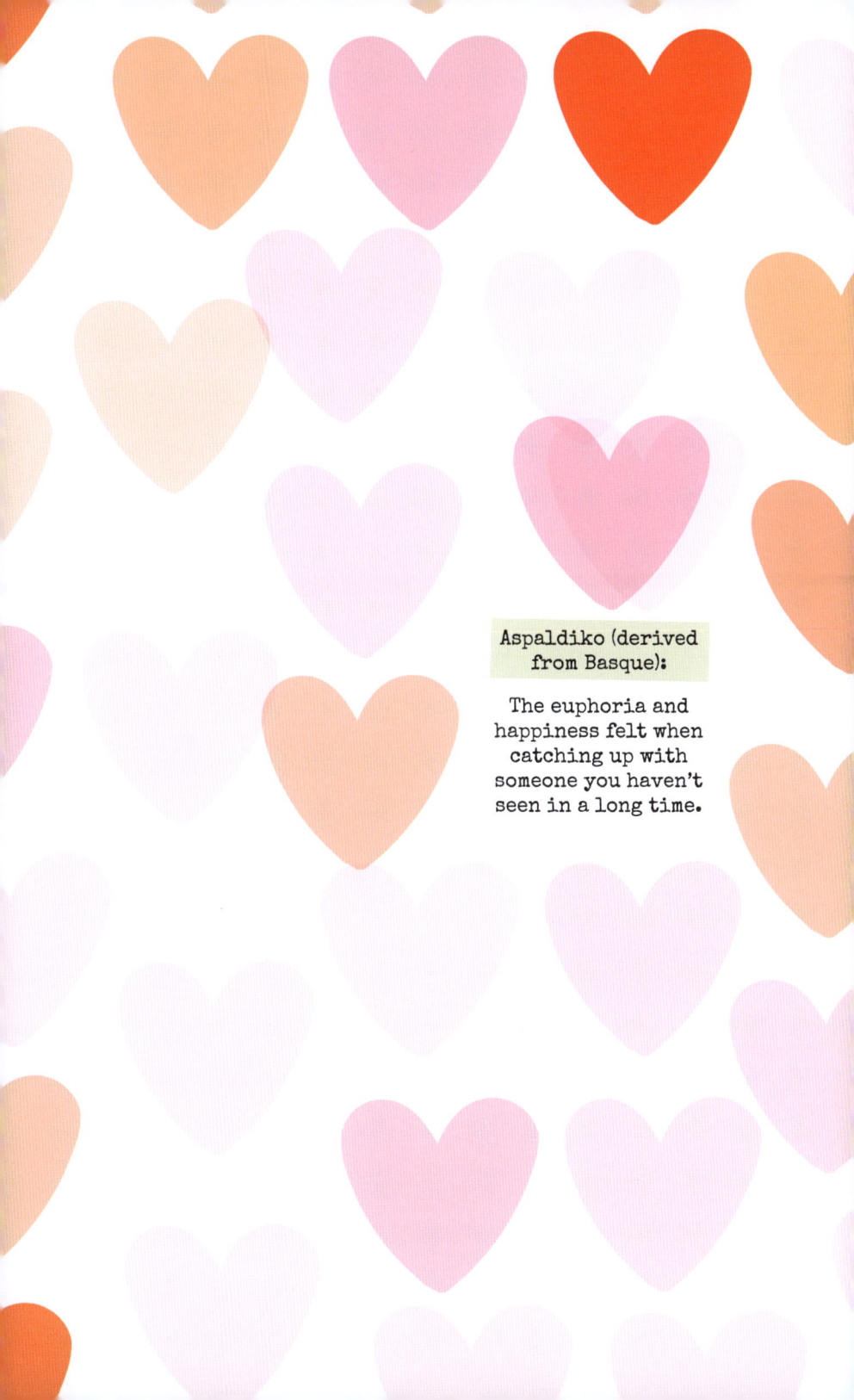

Aspaldiko (derived from Basque):

The euphoria and happiness felt when catching up with someone you haven't seen in a long time.

'A calm mind, a fit body, and a house full of LOVE. These things cannot be bought. They MUST be earned.'

x

(Naval Ravikant, author)

Love
is like
ketchup
– put it on
anything
and it tastes
better.

Love and learning

Ever wondered how love and learning are linked?

Kids ask, in this order:
Am I safe?
Am I loved?

If they can answer 'yes' to both, they move onto ...

Excellent! *NOW* I can learn!

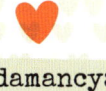

Redamancy:

Used in the 1600s to
mean the act of loving
the one who loves you.

Nowadays we call it
requited love, i.e., a
love returned in full.

Or, even better, feeling
all loved up!

A brainy SOS

Hi. It's your brain here. You've been ignoring my recent warnings so I'm going old school and writing you a letter instead. It might seem a little weird, but please go with it. What follows is a heartfelt message from me (your brain) to you (your body) because life's phenomenal when we work together.

Dear body,

I've been trying to grab your attention by making you lethargic and irritable. You know when you slump out of bed in a grump, that's me sending you a warning. This is a heartfelt SOS from your grey matter: *Help, I'm struggling!*

And if I'm struggling, you will be too! Because you and I (brain and body), for richer or poorer, better or worse, till death us do part ... we're lifelong partners. We need to work as a team.

Maybe you don't remember, but we've both always needed sleep. You used to sleep for 16 hours a day when you were a baby! Then, in primary school, your bedtime was 7 p.m. As we've gotten older you've started sleep cheating. It all kicked off when you got all those screens; 7 p.m. crept to 8, then 9. Then the smartphone appeared and your sleep patterns went haywire.

Here's something you probably don't know. When you're in the land of nod I take the opportunity to do some cleaning. During what's called your slow-wave sleep I open the brain/spinal fluid sluice gates and clear the waste.

It's true, I promise. Every single night, when you close your eyes, I rinse myself in a watery cerebrospinal fluid that flushes out toxic proteins and carries them to your liver where they're disposed of. Think of it like brain poop. It sounds a bit gross but when you're sleep-deprived you feel groggy and confused ... it's because you've got a head full of brain poop. You're clogged up with cranial constipation.

Good quality sleep is brainwashing, but in a good way! I can only clean your brain poop while you're asleep. In awake mode I'm crazy busy running your life: walking, talking, learning, thinking, feeling, calculating, reacting, anticipating – I've not got time to flush the brain poop.

Think of it like a house party. You can be in full-on party mode or you can clean up. It's hard to do both at the same time. So you party hard during the day, and then I clean up afterwards! That's how it works. Or at least, how it's *supposed* to work!

If you gave me more time, I could do a proper scrub and polish and you wouldn't be falling asleep in those morning meetings or be so damn grumpy with your partner.

Hey, I don't want to scare you but over time that brain poop can build up and stink the whole place out. If you're sleep cheating, it makes it harder for me to help you do super-important stuff like fighting cancer and other illnesses. Sleep should be an absolute #1 priority. It's clean and repair time.

So, a small request from me – can you remove all screens from the bedroom and leave your phone plugged in downstairs during the night? You might think listening to something helps you sleep but in reality all that background noise does is distract me from doing my job of cleaning things up.

Look, I'm your brain. I need you to help transport me around and you need me to help you be smart. It's a win-win deal. If you commit to getting a quality night's sleep every night (not just on the weekends), then I'll help you have an amazing life.

Here's the clincher – have you ever wondered why it's sometimes called 'beauty sleep'? Because sleep makes you happier, less anxious, smarter and even more attractive – *seriously!*

I love you, and getting our sleep right is the best way to love me, and yourself, back.

Yours cerebrally,

Your brain

LOVE horror-scopes

Good news. Love is written in the stars.

Bad news. *The stars don't always align!*

So here are our LOVE *horror*-scopes for the year ahead. It's cosmic nonsense for when things go horribly wrong.

ARIES (MAR 21 – APR 19)

You'll fall head-over-heels for someone this year – down two flights of stairs. *Ouch!*

Avoid last year's desperation (when you dated someone based entirely on their font choices) and play it cool. Cupid's loading his arrows so be ready, love is definitely coming. Possibly dressed as a parcel delivery driver.

TAURUS (APR 20 – MAY 20)

This year you'll discover that love isn't just about long walks on the beach. Sometimes it's about arguing over how to stack the dishwasher. Your soulmate may be closer than you think – possibly in the frozen veg aisle. Wear your best undies, just in case.

GEMINI (MAY 21 – JUN 20)
Love is a feral creature. It will ignore your rules, interrupt your routine and kiss you when you've got toothpaste on your chin. This is progress, Gemini.

CANCER (JUN 21 – JUL 22)
You're a hopeless romantic, which is lovely, but also a bit clingy. Try not to propose on the second date this year Cancer, and step away from the vision board.

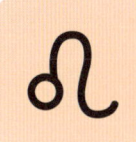

LEO (JUL 23 – AUG 22)
Hopelessly romantic, all Leos love love. But this year, you're advised to keep one foot in reality. Especially when dating people who say 'I'm between jobs' but live in a van. Aim for passion, not parole.

VIRGO (AUG 23 – SEP 22)
Virgos love a plan. But love isn't a spreadsheet, Virgo. You can't *Excel* your way into someone's heart. Let go of control and let romance surprise you. This could be the year you kiss someone *without* checking their credit score.

LIBRA (SEP 23 – OCT 22)

The stars point to a new direction. While it's true that dressing up is sexy and everyone swoons over a person in uniform, do not get over-excited about your new career at McDonalds.

SCORPIO (OCT 23 – NOV 21)

There's a saying along the lines of the good guy/gal always coming last, so forget niceness and rediscover your Scorpion sting. Hopefully this mean streak will get you noticed. But don't take it too far. Love will find you this year ... but so will a restraining order if you don't ease off the eye contact. The stars say: maybe try flirting that doesn't involve a death stare.

SAGITTARIUS (NOV 22 – DEC 21)

Time and space are both illusions, making it even more frustrating that you're always in the wrong place at the wrong time.

You're always chasing adventure, which is sexy – but this year, try staying still long enough to fall in love. Or at least long enough to finish your Tinder profile.

CAPRICORN (DEC 22 – JAN 19)

You've been practising your first name with their last name again, haven't you? The stars say *stop it.*

Love is serious business for you, Capricorn. But not everything needs a SWOT analysis. If someone flirts with you, maybe don't ask about their five-year plan.

AQUARIUS (JAN 20 – FEB 18)

You crave stability, cuddles, and carbs. Someone will try to win your heart with a salad. Don't trust them. They are *not* your person. Real love is someone who orders pudding and custard with two spoons. That's your soulmate.

PISCES (FEB 19 – MAR 20)

You've finally got your life together (congrats, your little yellow folders have little yellow folders in them) but your life will be turned upside down by something *un*-planned. This year someone spontaneous will derail your routine and leave coffee rings on your spreadsheet. Wake up and smell the fish, Pisces, it might be the best thing that ever happens to you.

LOVE books

Our final note is a thank you. Even if you're not here to stay, we're eternally grateful that the universe allowed your soul to stop by.

So just in case nobody's told you yet today how absolutely, positively, incredibly amazing you are, we're telling you right now.

You are truly radiant.

Remember, we love you. *Unconditionally.*

That will be all for today.

Thank you for reading LOVE NOTES.

Now pass it on to someone spesh.

x

"I adore YOU, you CRAZY, GORGEOUS, wonderful (but also sometimes quite WEIRD - BUT also still very lovely) person"

Will Grayson

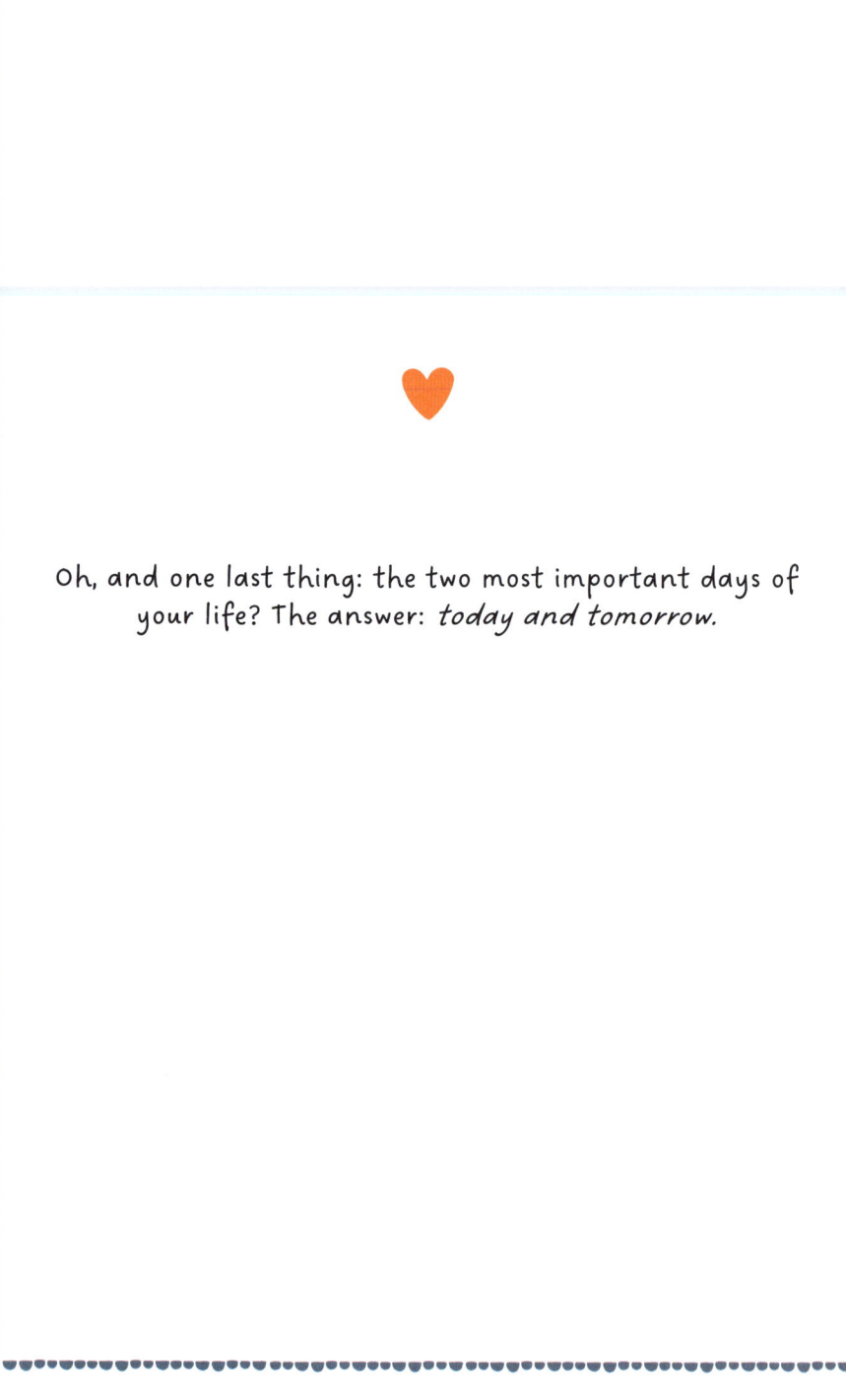

Oh, and one last thing: the two most important days of your life? The answer: *today and tomorrow.*

About the writing team

Amy Bradley

IN A WORD: Arty

Amy works from a small studio in Uttoxeter where she draws pictures for a living.

I know! Who knew that was an actual job!

Amy's worked on dozens of books, as well as postcards, posters and a range of amazing greetings cards that are almost too good to send. Her Art of Brilliance job title – 'Chief Social Media Guru and Designer of all Things Lush and Wonderful' – comes with one main responsibility: TO MAKE THE WORLD A BRIGHTER PLACE.

Amy's spare time is mostly spent eating cake and then running it off via half marathons.

Hannah Knowles

IN A WORD: Active

When Hannah isn't delivering workshops and keynotes for Art of Brill, she's busy being a mum to Daisy, devouring books like they're a food group, or pushing her limits in endurance events like Ironman.

Hannah specialises in positive psychology and all the fascinating subjects it encompasses. So if you want training or a keynote on well-being, change, confidence, happiness, potential, resilience (or more), she's ready, willing and promises it will knock your socks off.

LOVE NOTES is Hannah's first book and she couldn't be more excited to share it with you.

Andy Cope

IN A WORD: <mark>Lucky</mark>

Going by the moniker 'Dr of Happiness', Andy is really milking his PhD in human flourishing. Breezing through life with an air of *not taking himself too seriously*, Andy delivers keynotes all over the world.

Described by his mum as 'Not even the best writer in this family', Andy has amassed a decent back catalogue. He started his writing career in children's fiction (his Spy Dog series has sold a million copies worldwide) before moving into personal development and self-help. He's written lots of books, including *The Art of Being Brilliant*, *LADULT* and *Diary of a Brilliant Kid*, but never anything quite as gorgeous as this one.

ALSO AVAILABLE BY
ANDY COPE

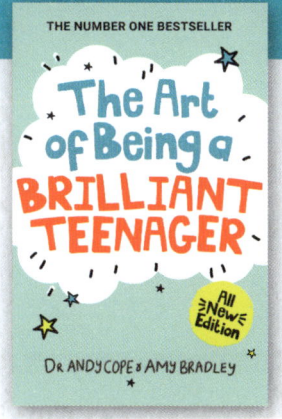

9780857089397
**The Art of Being
A Brilliant Teenager**

9781907326073
Ladult

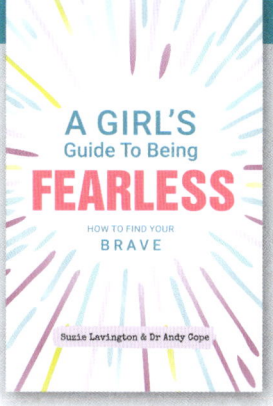

9780857088574
**A Girl's Guide
to Being Fearless**

9780857087867
Diary of a Brilliant Kid

9780857088918
Brill Kid - The Big Number 2

AVAILABLE WHEREVER
BOOKS ARE SOLD

ALSO AVAILABLE BY
ANDY COPE

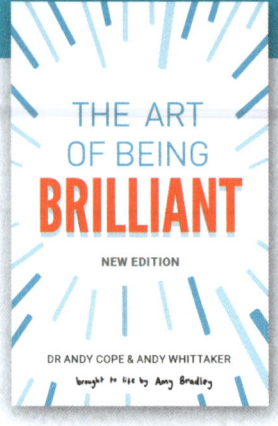

9780857089861
The Art of Being Brilliant

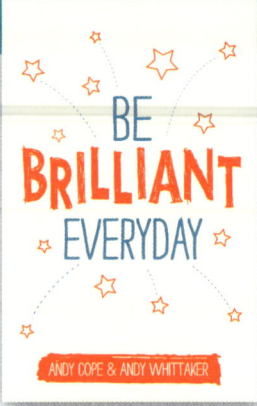

9780857085009
Be Brilliant Every Day

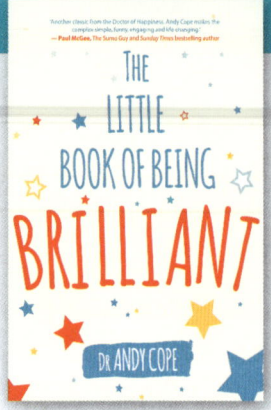

9780857087973
The Little Book of Being Brilliant

9780857087652
Shine

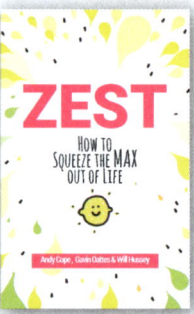

9780857088000
Zest

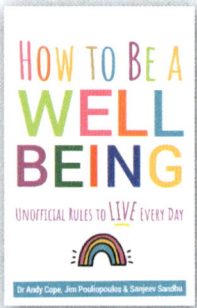

9780857088673
How to Be a Well Being

9780857088888
The Happiness Revolution

AVAILABLE WHEREVER
BOOKS ARE SOLD